DATE L...

Get Updates and More on Nolo.com

Go to this book's companion page at:

www.nolo.com/back-of-book/QPAT.html

When there's an important change to the law affecting this book, we'll post updates. You'll also find articles and other related materials.

More Resources
from Nolo.com

Legal Forms, Books, & Software
Hundreds of do-it-yourself products—all written in plain English, approved, and updated by our in-house legal editors.

Legal Articles
Get informed with thousands of free articles on everyday legal topics. Our articles are accurate, up to date, and reader friendly.

Find a Lawyer
Want to talk to a lawyer? Use Nolo to find a lawyer who can help you with your case.

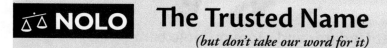

The Trusted Name
(but don't take our word for it)

"In Nolo you can trust."
THE NEW YORK TIMES

"Nolo is always there in a jam as the nation's premier publisher of do-it-yourself legal books."
NEWSWEEK

"Nolo publications…guide people simply through the how, when, where and why of the law."
THE WASHINGTON POST

"[Nolo's]…material is developed by experienced attorneys who have a knack for making complicated material accessible."
LIBRARY JOURNAL

"When it comes to self-help legal stuff, nobody does a better job than Nolo…"
USA TODAY

"The most prominent U.S. publisher of self-help legal aids."
TIME MAGAZINE

"Nolo is a pioneer in both consumer and business self-help books and software."
LOS ANGELES TIMES

10th Edition

Nolo's Patents
for Beginners

**Patent Agent David Pressman
and Attorney Richard Stim**

TENTH EDITION	JUNE 2021
Editor	DIANA FITZPATRICK
Cover Design	SUSAN PUTNEY
Book Design	SUSAN PUTNEY
Proofreading	JOCELYN TRUITT
Index	THÉRÈSE SHERE
Printing	BANG PRINTING

ISSN 2767-3596 (print)

ISSN 2767-360X (online)

ISBN 978-1-4133-2868-4 (pbk)

ISBN 978-1-4133-2869-1 (ebook)

This book covers only United States law, unless it specifically states otherwise.

Acknowledgments

We would like to thank our editor, Diana Fitzpatrick, and the staff at Nolo.

About the Authors

David Pressman is the author of *Patent It Yourself* (Nolo) and has had more than 40 years' experience in the patent profession as a patent examiner for the U.S. Patent Office; a patent attorney for Philco-Ford Corp., Elco Corp., and Varian Associates; as a columnist for *EDN* Magazine; and as an instructor at San Francisco State University. He contributed the Patent, Trademark, and Copyright entries to the *World Book Encyclopedia*. He's also an inventor with two patents issued. When not writing, dabbling in electronics, programming, inventing, or playing his trumpet, he practices as a patent agent in San Francisco. Originally from Philadelphia, he has a B.S. in Electrical Engineering from Pennsylvania State University. He completed his first year in law school at the University of Pennsylvania and the remaining years at George Washington University, where he served on the Law Review and received a Juris Doctor degree. He is also active in the general semantics and vegetarian movements.

Richard Stim is the author of several Nolo books, including *Music Law: How to Run Your Band's Business* and *Patent Pending in 24 Hours*.

Table of Contents

Your Legal Companion

The title of this book may have you wondering. Can patents—an area of law filled with arcane terminology, strange rules, and scientific jargon—really be reduced to a beginner's level? Don't fear. We're convinced that with a little diligence, anyone can understand the basics of patent law.

Keep in mind that the major principle underlying patent protection has not changed since 1790. If you devise something new and it qualifies for a patent, you can, for a limited time, prevent anyone else from making, selling, or using it. However, the technological changes of the past 25 years have dramatically altered the patent landscape. The number of utility patent applications has nearly tripled since 1980. In all, more than ten million patents have been granted since the United States began its patent program in 1790. (Patent numbering didn't begin until 1836.)

Patents are now considered an integral part of a corporation's strategic business plan. And this strategy is not limited to corporate boardrooms. For example, the total revenue for university patents has gone from less than one million dollars in 1980 to more than half a billion dollars today.

The patent system has also become far more accessible than it was two decades ago. You can now search patent records at the U.S. Patent and Trademark Office (PTO), on Google, or at many other websites. Patent forms and rules can now be easily downloaded, and patents and other documentation can be filed online.

To stay current with the modern world of patents, we have created a compact modern patent guide that explains patent law and provides clear instructions for deciphering and searching for patents. This book is intended for use by inventors, educators, entrepreneurs, students, non-patent attorneys, and businesspeople who must deal with and understand basic principles of patent law.

Chapters are organized into four categories: basic patent principles, rules for documenting and acquiring patent rights, patent ownership and disputes, and international patent law (Chapter 10 provides helpful resources):

- **Principles of patent law.** The first two chapters explain basic patent principles, the types of patents, the innovations that can and cannot be protected, novelty, nonobviousness, and the statutory standards for patent protection.

- **Documenting, searching, and prosecuting patents.** Chapter 3 describes invention documentation. Chapter 4 describes patent searching, and Chapter 5 describes how to read and write a patent application. Chapter 6 describes patent prosecution—the process of shepherding the patent application through the PTO.

- **Ownership and patent disputes.** Chapter 7 provides information about ownership rights (for example, how inventors claim joint ownership and its implications). Chapter 8 focuses on the issues of litigating patent disputes and standards for patent infringement.

- **International law.** Chapter 9 provides rules for international patent protection.

- **Resources.** We have provided a Glossary to assist in deciphering patent law. Additionally, Chapter 10 offers additional inventor and patent resources.

An instructor using the book as a teaching tool can proceed systematically through the chapters beginning with principles of protection, followed by patent application principles, and culminating with patent disputes and international patent law. For students, the material includes current case law, references, and examples.

Get Updates and More Online

When there are important changes to the information in this book, we'll post updates online, on a page dedicated to this book:

www.nolo.com/back-of-book/QPAT.html

Patents and Intellectual Property Law

Our nation rewards inventors by giving them a limited monopoly over the sale and manufacture of their inventions. For example, in the 19th century, one company controlled the manufacture and sale of all matches, while another company controlled the manufacture and sale of all safety pins. Matches and safety pins, just like paper clips and ballpoint pens, may seem obvious now, but once they were novel discoveries protected by patent laws. Eventually all patents expire, and as a result, now any company can manufacture and sell matches and safety pins without seeking permission.

This chapter will introduce you to some patent basics and summarize patent standards. Since patents are a member of the intellectual property family, we will also introduce principles of copyrights, trademarks, and trade secrets.

What Is a Patent?

A "patent" is a grant from the federal government that gives an inventor the right to exclude others from making, using, selling, importing, or offering an invention for sale for a fixed period of time. For example, Whitcomb Judson received a patent in 1893 for the zipper, and for 17 years, Judson alone was entitled to manufacture and sell this invention.

"Invention" has a broad meaning. It is any new article, machine, composition, process, or new use developed by a human. For example, in 1988 Drs. Leder and Stewart (on behalf of Harvard University) were issued the first patent for a new animal life form embodied in a genetically altered mouse that was more susceptible to cancer. This new life form is an invention and was awarded a patent.

The patent right lasts for 20 years from the date the application was filed (approximately 17 to 18 years from the date the patent issues, provided three maintenance fees are paid). After the patent right ends, anyone can freely copy the invention.

A patent is a form of personal property and can be sold outright for a lump sum, or its owner can give anyone permission to use the invention ("license it") in return for royalty payments. A patent can also be transferred by gift, will, or descent under a state's intestate succession (no-will) laws.

Definitions, Case Law, and Statutes

We define many terms throughout this book, and these definitions are collected in the Glossary at the end of this book. We also provide references to lawsuits and statutes. You can recognize the reference to lawsuits because the names are in italics, usually separated by a "v."; for example, *Diamond v. Chakrabarty*, 447 U.S. 303 (1980). The information following the names refers to volume, book, and page number where the case is located. The citation system is beyond the scope of this book, but if you are interested in doing further legal research, read *Legal Research: How to Find & Understand the Law*, by Stephen Elias and the Editors of Nolo (Nolo). A statute is another form of legal citation and is recognizable by the use of a section mark ("§"). For example, "35 U.S.C. § 161" refers to Section 161 of Title 35 of the U.S. Code (U.S.C.). Title 35 contains the patent laws. The U.S.C. can be found in most law libraries and online, and the entire patent code is available at the U.S. Patent and Trademark Office website, www.uspto.gov.

The Three Types of Patents

There are three types of patents—utility patents, design patents, and plant patents.

Utility Patents. A utility patent, the most common type of patent, covers inventions that function in a unique manner to produce a utilitarian result. Examples of utility inventions are Velcro fasteners, new vaccines, electronic circuits, software, semiconductor manufacturing processes, new bacteria, new animals, plants, automatic transmissions, and virtually anything else under the sun that can be made by humans. This book is devoted primarily to utility patents.

Design Patents. A design patent covers the unique, ornamental, or visible shape or design of a useful object. Thus, if a lamp, building, phone case, or desk has a truly unique appearance, its design can be patented. Even the icons that appear on your phone or computer screen can be patented. However, the uniqueness of the design must be purely ornamental or aesthetic; if the shape is functional and aesthetic, then only a utility patent is proper. A useful way to distinguish between a design and a utility invention is to ask, "Will removing the novel features substantially affect the function of the device?" For example, removing the carved wood design in the headboard of a bed would not affect how the bed functioned and these carvings could be protected as a design patent. On the other hand, a baseball bat and fishing rod may have pleasing designs but unless they have nonfunctional aesthetic features, their shape is purely functional and suitable only for a utility patent. (For more information on design patents, see Chapter 2.)

Plant Patents. A plant patent covers plants that can be reproduced through the use of grafts and cuttings, such as flowers. These are referred to as asexually reproducible plants. (35 U.S.C. § 161.) The Plant Variety Protection Act covers those plants that use pollination (sexually reproducible plants). (7 U.S.C. § 2321.) Under some circumstances, utility patents can cover sexually and asexually reproducible plants. (For more information on plant patents, see Chapter 2.)

Patent Rights

A patent gives its owner the right to sue infringers, that is, anyone who imports, makes, uses, sells, or offers the invention for sale (or an essential part of it) without authorization. If the patent owner wins the lawsuit, the judge will issue a signed order (an "injunction") against the infringer, ordering the infringer not to make, use, or sell the invention. The judge will also award the patent owner damages—money to compensate the patent owner for loss due to the infringement. The amount of the damages is often equivalent to a reasonable royalty (say, 5% of revenues), based on the infringer's sales. However, if the patent owner can convince the judge that the infringer acted in bad faith—for example, infringed intentionally with no reasonable excuse—the judge can triple the damages and make the infringer pay the patent owner's attorneys' fees. (For more information on patent infringement, see Chapter 8.)

Offensive Rights—Not Protection

Many people refer to patents as a form of "protection." However, patents don't provide any defensive "protection" in their own right. A patent is an offensive weapon. For example, patent ownership, by itself, will not necessarily keep anyone from copying your invention and violating your patent rights. However, as a patent owner, you can successfully sue or threaten to sue anyone who wrongfully trespasses on those rights. The distinction between defensive and offensive rights is as important in intellectual property law as it is in football or basketball: While a good defense may be valuable, the patent owner will need to use the patent's powerful offense to win the game or stop the infringer.

Patent rights extend throughout the entire United States, its territories, and possessions. Under international treaties, the owner of a U.S. patent can acquire patent rights in other countries by filing corresponding patent applications abroad as outlined in Chapter 9. Congress derives its power to make the patent statutes from the U.S. Constitution (Art. 1, § 8). The statutes, in turn, authorize the PTO to issue its Rules of Practice and its *Manual of Patent Examining Procedure* (MPEP).

The Requirements for Obtaining a Patent

An inventor applies for the patent by filing a patent application, a set of papers that describes an invention. The Patent and Trademark Office (PTO) is a division of the Department of Commerce. A patent examiner at the PTO must be convinced that the invention satisfies the "novelty" and "nonobviousness" requirements of the patent laws.

The novelty requirement is easy to satisfy: The invention must be different from what is already known to the public. Any difference, however slight, will suffice. In addition to being novel, the examiner must also be convinced that the invention is nonobvious (or unobvious). This means that at the time the inventor came up with the invention, it would not have been considered obvious to a person skilled in the technology (called "art"). Nonobviousness is best shown by new and unexpected, surprising, or far superior results, when compared to previous inventions and knowledge ("prior art") in the particular area of the invention. In addition to being novel and unobvious, utility inventions must also meet other legal requirements. More on this in Chapter 2.

We discuss the patent application process and the PTO in more detail in Chapters 5 and 6, and information about the PTO can be accessed online at www.uspto.gov or by writing to the Commissioner for Patents, P.O. Box 1450, Alexandria, VA 22313.

How Long Do Patent Rights Last?

Until 1995, utility patents were granted for a period of 17 years, assuming required maintenance fees were paid. However, as a result of a change in patent laws, utility and plant patents issuing from applications filed after June 7, 1995 will expire 20 years from the date of filing. Certain utility patents will be extended to compensate for the following:

- delays resulting from the failure of the PTO to examine a new application within 14 months of filing
- delays caused by the PTO's failure to issue a patent within three years from filing, unless the delay was caused or instigated by the inventor, and
- delays caused by the PTO's failure to take certain office actions for more than four months.

In addition, patent rights may be extended for certain products whose commercial marketing has been delayed due to regulatory review, such as for drugs or food additives. (35 U.S.C. §§ 155–156.)

The term for design patents is 15 years from the date the patent is issued (the "date of issue"). (If filed before May 13, 2015, the design patent lasts 14 years from date of issue.)

From the date of filing to date of issuance (the "pendency period") the inventor has no patent rights, with one exception: If the application has been published and the applicant notified an infringer of the published application, the applicant may later (after the patent issues) seek royalties for infringement during the postpublication pendency period. In any case, when and if the patent later issues, the inventor will obtain the right to prevent the continuation of any infringing activity that started during the pendency period. Patents aren't renewable, and once patented, an invention may not be repatented.

How Patent Rights Can Be Lost

Patent rights can be lost if any of the following applies:

- Fees required to keep the patent in force (known as "maintenance fees") aren't paid (see Chapter 6).
- It can be proved that the patent doesn't (a) adequately explain how to make and use the invention, (b) improperly describes the invention, or (c) contains claims that are inadequate (see Chapter 5).
- One or more earlier patents or other publications (prior-art references) are uncovered that show that the invention wasn't new or wasn't different enough to qualify for patent rights (see Chapter 4).
- The patent owner engages in certain defined types of illegal conduct, that is, commits antitrust or other violations connected with the patent (see Chapter 8).
- The patent applicant committed "fraud on the Patent and Trademark Office (PTO)" by failing to disclose material information, such as relevant prior-art references, to the PTO during the period when the patent application was pending (see Chapter 8).

In short, the patent monopoly, while powerful, may be defeated and is limited in scope and time.

Intellectual Property—The Big Picture

Intellectual property refers to any product of the human mind or intellect, such as an idea, invention, artistic expression, unique name, business method, industrial process, or chemical formula. Intellectual property (IP) law determines when and how a person can capitalize on a creation. Intellectual property law has several subcategories, based on the type of "property" involved:

- **Patent law** deals with the protection of inventions.
- **Trademark law** deals with the protection of a brand name, design, slogan, sound, smell, or any other symbol used to identify and market goods or services. Examples of trademarks are the words "Ivory," "Coke," and "Nolo," as well as the Tesla ("T") logo, and the Mister Softee musical jingle.
- **Copyright law** deals with the protection of books, movies, music, visual works and other forms of personal expression, giving the creator the right to prevent others from copying or using their works without permission and to recover damages from those who do so.
- **Trade secret law** protects confidential business information that gives a business an advantage over its competitors—for example, manufacturing processes, magic tricks, and drink formulae.
- **Unfair competition law** permits a business to sue over certain types of unethical behavior by competitors. For example, if a company claims to be an authorized "Apple" reseller but is not; or if a car company imitates a singer's unique vocal style in a car commercial to imply the singer endorses the car.

Trademarks

On a daily basis, everyone sees, uses, and makes many decisions on the basis of trademarks, making them the most familiar branch of intellectual property law. For instance, the purchase of a car, an appliance, packaged food, a magazine, a smartphone, or a watch is based, at least to some extent, on the trademark.

What Is a Trademark?

In its most literal meaning, a trademark is any word or other symbol that is consistently associated with a product or service and identifies and distinguishes that product or service from others in the marketplace. A trademark can be a word (Apple), a design or logo (the Nike swoosh), a sound (the MGM lion's roar), shapes (the truncated, contrasting, conical top of Cross pens), colors (and color combinations), and even smells. The term "trademark" is also commonly used to mean "service marks." These are marks (words or other symbols) that are associated with services offered in the marketplace. The word HULU in connection with the streaming network is one example of a service mark. Another is the emblem used by Blue Cross–Blue Shield for its medical insurance services.

Trademark Rights and Registration

The trademark owner can prevent another business from using the same or a confusingly similar mark for the same or similar goods. Owners of famous marks can prevent the use of similar marks that dilute or tarnish the trademark's image, even if these uses are not on similar goods or services.

Contrary to popular belief, trademarks do not have to be registered for offensive rights to be acquired (although registration can substantially add to the trademark owner's rights). Trademark rights are acquired by the first person to actually use the trademark in commerce or file an intent-to-use (ITU) application to register the trademark and subsequently use the mark in commerce. Actual use in commerce means shipping goods or advertising services in interstate or foreign commerce that bear the trademark.

Relationship of Trademark Law to Patent Law

Trademarks are useful in conjunction with inventions, whether patentable or not. For example, consider the Crock Pot and the Hula Hoop. Both of these products were unpatentable, but the names of the products were protected under trademark laws. As a result of advertising, consumers sought out the trademarked products and not those from competitors. In short, a trademark provides brand name recognition to the product and a patent provides a tool to enforce a monopoly based on functional features. Because trademark rights can be kept forever (as long as the trademark continues to be used), a trademark can be a means of extending a monopoly long after the patent has expired. For example, the Scotchgard process for protecting carpets was invented by Patsy Sherman and Samuel Smith and patented in 1973. Even though other companies may now copy the process, the Scotchgard trademark is still synonymous with quality carpet protection and gives the company an edge among consumers who want products to protect carpet and fabrics.

RESOURCE

For more information on federal trademarks, access the U.S. Patent and Trademark Office at www.uspto.gov, or review *Trademark: Legal Care for Your Business & Product Name,* by Stephen Fishman (Nolo).

Trade Names Versus Trademarks

Trade names are used to identify business entities, whereas trademarks are used to identify products and services produced by such entities. Under the Lanham Act, a trade name is the name of any commercial firm, association, corporation, company, or other organization capable of suing and being sued in a court of law. Trade names cannot be registered under the trademark and service mark provisions of the Lanham Act. However, they are entitled to protection under the unfair competition provision of the Lanham Act. (15 U.S.C. § 1125.) They are also protected under state unfair competition statutes and court decisions, if the public is likely to be confused by the use of the same or a similar name. Companies frequently use their trade names as trademarks or service marks for their products and services—that is, as designators of origin in their advertising and on the products. For instance, Apple Computer Corporation uses the trade name "Apple" as a trademark, and the McDonald's fast food chain uses "McDonald's" as a service mark. In these situations, the trade name may be registered in its capacity as a mark and may receive additional protection under the Lanham Act's provisions applicable to infringement of marks.

Copyright

Some specific types of works that are covered by copyright are books, poetry, plays, songs, catalogs, photographs, software, advertisements, labels, movies, maps, drawings, sculpture, prints and art reproductions, board games and rules, and recordings.

What Is a Copyright?

Copyright is a legal right given to an author, artist, composer, or programmer, to exclude others from publishing or copying literary, dramatic, musical, artistic, or software works. A copyright covers only the author's or artist's particular way of expressing an idea, not the idea per se. While a copyright can provide offensive rights on the particular arrangement of words that constitute a book or play, it can't cover the book's subject matter, message, or teachings. For example, you are free to publish any of the ideas, concepts, and information in this (or any) book, provided that you use your own words. But if you copy the specific wording, then you have likely infringed the copyright on this book.

To obtain a copyright, a work must be "original," not merely the result of extended effort. For example, a telephone company that compiled, through much work, an alphabetical directory of names and addresses could not prevent another publisher from copying the directory, because there was no originality in an alphabetized list of phone customers. Certain items, such as a title, short phrase, lettering, an idea, a plan, a form, a system, a method, a process, a concept, a principle, and a device can't be protected by copyright. U.S. government publications aren't covered by copyright and may almost always be freely copied. Aesthetic features of a useful article can be protected by copyright law—provided that the art can be separated from and can exist independently of the article (known as the "separability requirement"). For example, copyright cannot protect a belt buckle but can protect a design that is affixed to the buckle.

Rights and Registration

The copyright springs into existence the instant the work of expression first assumes some tangible form, for example, once a song is recorded or a book is written. Copyright lasts for the life of the author plus 70 years, or for works made for hire, 95 years from publication or 120 years from creation, whichever is shorter. A work made for hire is one made by an employee in the course of the employment or by an independent contractor under a written work-made-for-hire contract. The copyright owner in a work made for hire is the hiring party or employer.

Registration is not necessary to acquire copyright, but if a work is registered within three months of the time the work is distributed or published, or before the infringement occurs, it may entitle the copyright owner to attorneys' fees, costs, and damages that don't have to be proved (called "statutory damages").

TIP

Copyright notice. While no longer necessary for works published after March 1, 1989, it's still advisable to place the familiar copyright notice (for example, "Copyright © 2021 David Pressman") on each published copy of the work. This tells anyone who sees the work that the copyright is being claimed, who is claiming it, and when the work was first published. This notice prevents an infringer from later claiming that the infringement was accidental.

Copyright Compared With Utility Patents

Things that are entitled to a patent are generally not entitled to copyright, and vice versa. Assuming they don't have any aesthetic components, patents are exclusive for machines, compositions, articles of manufacture, processes, and new uses. On the other hand, copyrights are exclusive for works of expression, such as writings, movies, plays, recordings, and artwork, assuming they don't have any functional aspects. However, a few creations may be eligible for both types of coverage (see "Computer Software," below).

In many areas, both forms of coverage can be used together for different aspects of a creation. For instance, in a board game, the game apparatus, if sufficiently unique, can be patented, while the gameboard, rules, box, and design of the game pieces can be covered by copyright. The artwork on the box or package for almost any invention can be covered by copyright, as can the instructions accompanying the product. Also the name of the game (for example, Dungeons and Dragons) is a trademark and can be covered as such.

Copyright Compared With Design Patents

There's considerable overlap here, because aesthetics are the basis of both forms of coverage. Design patents are used mainly to cover industrial designs where the shape of the object has ornamental features and the shape is inseparable from, or meaningless if separated from, the object. For example, a tire tread design and a computer case are perfect for design patents. However, a surface decal, which could be used elsewhere, is not.

Computer Software

Viewed one way, computer programs are nothing more than a series of numerical relationships (termed "routines") and as such cannot qualify for a patent, although they can be covered under the copyright laws because they constitute a creative work of expression. However, viewed from another perspective, computer programs are a set of instructions that make a machine (the computer) operate in a certain way. Software that qualifies is registrable as a utility patent. However, the future of software patents has been unclear following the Supreme Court's decision in *Alice Corp. v. CLS Bank Int'l* (134 S. Ct. 2347 (2014).) In *Alice*, the Court held that merely computerizing a conventional process is not patentable and that software that claimed an abstract idea would not be protected. (Unfortunately, the Court did not define what it meant by the term "abstract" in this context.) This decision cast a cloud on software patents. Also, keep in mind that the ease with which copyright is obtained must be counterbalanced by the narrow nature of its coverage.

Copyright, on the other hand, can be used for almost any artistic or written creation, whether or not it's inseparable from an underlying object, so long as the aspect of the work for which copyright is being sought is ornamental and not functional. This means copyright can be used for pure surface ornamentation, such as the artwork on a can of beans, as well as sculptural works where the "art" and the object are integrated, such as a statue. For instance, the shape of a toy was held to be properly covered by copyright because the shape played no role in how the toy functioned and a toy wasn't considered to perform a useful function (although most parents who use toys to divert their children would disagree).

Compared to copyright, design patents are relatively expensive and time-consuming to obtain and the rights last only 15 years. However, a design patent offers broader rights than a copyright in that it covers the aesthetic principles underlying the design. This means that someone else coming up with a similar, but somewhat changed design would probably be liable for design patent infringement. Also, to prove infringement of a copyrighted work, the copyright owner must show, by direct evidence or inference, that the accused copied the work. However no proof of copying is needed to prove infringement of a patent; independent creators are just as guilty as copiers.

RESOURCE

For more information on copyright, read *The Copyright Handbook: What Every Writer Needs to Know,* by Stephen Fishman. Also, the Copyright Office, Washington, D.C. 20559, provides free information and copyright forms at www.loc.gov.

Trade Secrets

Here we provide a basic definition of trade secrets, distinguish trade secret protection from patents, list the advantages and disadvantages of trade secret versus patenting, and explain how to acquire and maintain trade secret rights.

What Is a Trade Secret?

A trade secret is any information, design, device, process, composition, technique, or formula that is not known generally and that affords its owner a competitive business advantage. Examples of trade secrets are a chemical formula, a manufacturing process, a "magic-type" secret (such as techniques used to produce laser light shows and fireworks), and a recipe. Because these types of information and know-how go to the very heart of a business's competitive position, businesses expend a great deal of time, energy, and money to guard their trade secrets.

Acquiring and Maintaining Trade Secret Rights

The trade secret owner must take reasonable precautions to keep the information confidential in order to acquire and maintain trade secret rights. Also, an employer should have all employees who have access to company trade secrets sign an agreement to keep the information confidential. Over the years the courts have devised a number of tests for determining what these reasonable precautions should be and whether a trade secret owner has taken them. Most states now have a statute that makes the theft of a trade secret a criminal offense as well as the basis for civil lawsuit (for instance, the Uniform Trade Secrets Act, Cal. Civ. Code §§ 3246 and following).

There are two federal trade secret statutes: the Economic Espionage Act of 1996 (which criminalizes trade secret theft) and the Defend Trade Secrets Act of 2016 (DTSA), which provides a basis for trade secret owners to file civil lawsuits in federal court. Any company possessing a trade secret that is used in interstate or foreign commerce can take advantage of the provisions of the DTSA. Prior to the DTSA, trade secret owners could only bring civil lawsuits in state court, under state laws based on the Uniform Trade Secrets Act (UTSA). In many ways the DTSA and these state laws are similar, but the DTSA may be more favorable to trade secret owners since it provides access to federal courts, plus a method for seizing trade secrets without giving any notice to the defendant, an unprecedented leap from the notice requirements of state laws modeled on the UTSA.

Trade Secrets Compared With Patents

Assuming that an invention has been kept secret, an inventor can rely on trade secret principles to enforce rights on the invention. If an invention is maintained as a trade secret and put into commercial use, the inventor must file a patent application within one year of the date the invention was used commercially. If the inventor waits more than a year (and this fact is discovered), any patent that the inventor does ultimately obtain will be held invalid.

When a patent issues, the public has complete access to the ideas, techniques, approaches, and methods underlying the invention. This is because a patent application must clearly explain how to make and use the invention. Because the application is printed verbatim when the patent issues, all of this "know-how" becomes public. This public disclosure doesn't usually hurt the inventor, however, because once the patent is issued, the inventor can prevent anyone else from commercially exploiting the underlying information.

The PTO treats patent applications as confidential, so it is possible to apply for a patent and still maintain the underlying information as a trade secret during the patent application process, at least for the first 18 months.

Loss of Trade Secret Rights as a Result of 18-Month Publication Rule

U.S. patent applications are published 18 months after the earliest claimed filing date, unless the applicant files a Non-Publication Request (NPR) at the time of filing, stating that the application will not be filed abroad. If the applicant does file abroad, the NPR must be revoked. If the patent application is published but is later rejected, then the inventor is in the unfortunate position of having lost both trade secret and patent rights.

If an inventor files a patent application on an invention and the inventor wants to keep it as a trade secret if the patent isn't granted, the inventor will have to take steps to withdraw the application before publication to prevent loss of the trade secret rights. (See Chapter 6.) There is one advantage to publication in that an applicant whose application is published may obtain royalties from an infringer from the date of the publication if the application later issues as a patent. The infringer must have had actual notice of the publication. This can be accomplished by sending a copy of the publication to an infringer.

Advantages of Trade Secret Protection

Let's look at the reasons why some people choose trade secret rights over a patent:

- The main advantage of a trade secret is the possibility of perpetual protection. While a patent is limited by statute to 20 years from filing and isn't renewable, a trade secret will last indefinitely if not discovered. For example, some fireworks and sewing needle trade secrets have been maintained for decades.
- A trade secret can be maintained without the cost or effort involved in patenting.
- There is no need to disclose details of the invention to the public for trade secret rights (as the inventor has to do with a patented invention).
- With a trade secret, the inventor has definite, already existing rights and doesn't have to worry about whether the patent application will be allowed.
- Because a trade secret isn't distributed to the public as a patent is, no one can look at the trade secret and try to design around it, as they can with the claims of a patent.
- A trade secret can be established without naming any inventors, as must be done with a patent application. Thus no effort need be made to determine the proper inventor and, provided it has its employees sign the usual employment agreement, a company

needn't request its inventor-employee to assign (legally transfer) ownership of the trade secret to it, as is required with a patent application.

- A trade secret does not have to meet the novelty and nonobviousness requirements of a patent. In other words, it does not have to be as significant or important an advance as does a patented invention.
- A trade secret can cover more information, including many relatively minor details. A patent generally covers one broad principle and its ramifications. For example, a complicated manufacturing machine with many new designs and that incorporates several new techniques can be covered as a trade secret merely by keeping the whole machine secret. To cover it by patent, on the other hand, many expensive and time-consuming patent applications would be required, and even then the patent wouldn't cover many minor ideas in the machine.
- Trade secret rights are obtained immediately, whereas a patent takes a couple of years, in which time, rapidly evolving technology can bypass the patented invention.

Disadvantages of Trade Secret Protection

The main disadvantage of trade secrets is that protection is lost if the public learns the secret by inspecting, dissecting, or analyzing the product (called "reverse engineering"). Because very sophisticated analytic tools are now available, many objects and methods can be analyzed and copied, no matter how complex. And remember, the law generally allows anyone to copy and make anything freely, unless it is patented or subject to copyright protection.

Strict precautions must always be taken and continually enforced to maintain the confidentiality of a trade secret. If the trade secret is discovered legitimately (reverse engineered, accidentally posted on a company website, or by any other method), it's generally lost forever, although the trade secret owner does have rights against anyone who obtains the trade secret by illegal means.

A trade secret can be patented by someone else who discovers it by legitimate means. For instance, suppose an inventor creates a new formula for a hair treatment lotion, and someone who has never even heard of the lotion comes up with the same formula and patents it successfully. The patent owner can sue and hold the trade secret owner liable for infringing his or her patent! There is an exception: The owner of a patented process or method cannot obtain damages from a trade secret owner who was using the process or method more than a year before the patent's filing date. (See Chapter 8.)

 RESOURCE

For more information on trade secrets, consult *Nondisclosure Agreement for Inventors*, by Richard Stim, an eForm Kit available from www.nolo.com.

Unfair Competition

Unfair competition can be used to halt devious methods by which businesses act unfairly, including false advertising claims, false endorsement of products, deceptive packaging, and dishonest promotions or marketing. The scope of unfair competition law is nebulous in the first place and is regularly being changed by judges who make new and often contradictory rulings.

The primary federal law used to enforce unfair competition law is the federal "false designation of origin" statute. (15 U.S.C. § 1125(a).) If an injured party can prove that a business has engaged in unfair competition, a judge will issue an injunction (legal order) prohibiting the business from any further such activity or defining what the business can and can't do. Further, the court may award compensation (monetary damages) to the injured business (that is, the business that lost profits because of the public's confusion). Unfair competition occasionally intersects with patents. For example, a company may advertise it has a superior patented process for roach killing when it does not have a patent. A competitor can sue to stop the false advertising. ●

2

Qualifying for a Patent

ederal law sets four requirements for a utility patent. If an applicant fails to meet these requirements, the invention will not receive a patent. (More than half of all patent applications fail to acquire a patent.) In this chapter, we discuss the standards for utility patents, as well as design and plant patents, and we introduce an important concept known as "prior art."

Requirements for a Utility Patent

The PTO grants patent rights when four requirements are met:

1. **Statutory class.** The invention must fit into one of the classes established by Congress. (35 U.S.C. § 101.)
2. **Usefulness.** The invention must be useful. (35 U.S.C. § 101.)
3. **Novelty.** The invention must be novel. The invention must have an aspect that is different in some way from all previous knowledge and inventions. (35 U.S.C. § 102.)
4. **Nonobviousness.** The invention's novel features must not be obvious to someone who has ordinary skill in the specific technology involved in the invention. (35 U.S.C. § 103.)

Most inventions meet three of these standards; that is, they fit within at least one statutory class, have utility, and possess novelty. We have presented the four requirements in Fig. 2A as three upward steps as a reflection of this. The last requirement, nonobviousness, is represented by a relatively high step. That's because most of the inventions that fail to receive patents are rejected because the PTO believes the inventions are obvious.

Claims

Throughout this and other chapters, we refer to patent "claims." Claims are statements included in a patent application that describe (or "recite") the structure of an invention in precise and exact terms. Claims are essential because they set the boundaries of the inventor's rights. That is, claims define the extent of the patent protection for the invention. The drafting of patent claims is discussed in Chapter 5.

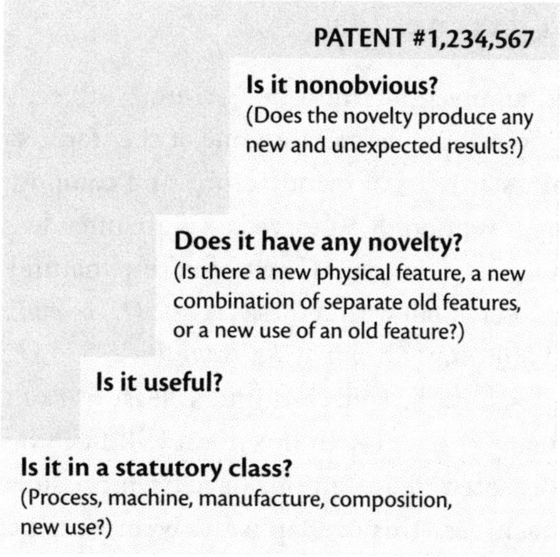

PATENT #1,234,567

Is it nonobvious?
(Does the novelty produce any
new and unexpected results?)

Does it have any novelty?
(Is there a new physical feature, a new
combination of separate old features,
or a new use of an old feature?)

Is it useful?

Is it in a statutory class?
(Process, machine, manufacture, composition,
new use?)

Figure 2A—Patentability Mountain
The Four Legal Requirements for Getting a Utility Patent

Inventor's Status—AI Need Not Apply

In discussing the requirements for obtaining a patent, we do not mention the inventor's status or personal qualifications because these are irrelevant. The applicant must qualify as a true inventor of the invention (discussed in Chapter 7), and personal qualities such as age, sex, citizenship, country of residence, mental competence, health, physical disabilities, incarceration, nationality, race, creed, and religion are irrelevant. Even dead or insane persons may apply through their representatives. Similarly, the manner of making an invention is irrelevant to patentability. A child who discovers something by accident is treated the same as a genius who comes up with the idea through years of hard work. However, one thing is clear. The inventor must be a person. In 2020, the PTO issued a decision stating that inventorship under U.S. patent law is limited to natural persons and rejecting an application for an invention by DABUS, an AI (artificial intelligence) machine.

Statutory Classes

To be patentable, an invention must be "statutory subject matter." This means that the invention must fall into one of the statutory classes—processes, machines, articles of manufacture, and compositions, or new use of an existing invention. Statutory classes are intended to encompass anything that is made by humans. Laws of nature, natural phenomena, and abstract ideas do not fall within these classes. (*Diamond v. Chakrabarty*, 447 U.S. 303 (1980); *Alice Corp. v. CLS Bank Int'l*, 573 U.S. 208 (2014).)

Most inventions can be squeezed into at least one of the statutory classes, and in many instances, an invention will fit into more than one. For example, software inventions have been classified as both processes and machines. This overlap is rarely an issue because a patent applicant is not required to specify the class to which an invention belongs. If the examiner feels that the invention isn't classifiable, the inventor must show into which class the invention falls. Below, we discuss the statutory classes in more detail.

Statutory Classes: Processes

A process (also known as a method) is a series of actions or steps that produce a result—for example, the steps required to create or administer a new vaccine. As the Supreme Court stated, "[A process] is an act, or a series of acts, performed upon the subject-matter to be transformed and reduced to a different state or thing." (*Gottschalk v. Benson*, 409 U.S. 63, 70 (1972).) In recent years, the process classification has been dominated by conventional processes, software inventions, and business method patents.

Conventional processes. Examples of conventional processes might include a recipe, a heat process, a chemical reaction, a medical procedure, the instructions for an IKEA table, a method for applying plaster, or the steps for attaching a hair piece to a bald person's head (using scalp sutures).

Software processes. Most software inventions are claimed as processes (a software program may also fall in the machine class). To be classified as a process, a software program must affect some hardware or process or produce a useful, concrete, and tangible result. Examples include a program that analyzes EKG, spectrographic, seismic, or data bit signals; controls a milling machine; creates images on a computer screen; formats the printing of mathematical formulae; submits bids for a service online; calculates mutual fund values; or recognizes patterns or voices.

Business method patents. Since 1998—when the Court of Appeals for the Federal Circuit (CAFC) ruled that a software process that calculated mutual fund investments was valid—the USPTO has granted patent protection for methods of doing business. (*State Street Bank & Trust Co. v. Signature Financial Group, Inc.*, 149 F.3d 1368 (Fed. Cir. 1998).) Before that ruling, software could only be patented if the software resulted in some physical activity. These patents are referred to as business method patents and were popularized by Amazon.com's "one-click" patent (for an express method of ordering merchandise online).

In 2010, software and business method patents became subject to higher scrutiny when the Supreme Court held that a business method for hedging risks in commodities trading was not patentable because it was an abstract idea. (*In re Bilski*, 200 U.S. 321 (2010).) Most software and business method patents' patentability was further placed in doubt when the U.S. Supreme Court decided *Alice Corp. v. CLS Bank Int'l*, 573 U.S. 208 (2014). At issue was a patent directed to a process for lessening settlement risk in a financial transaction by using a computer as a third-party intermediary. The Court held that the claims were invalid because they were directed to an "abstract" idea. The unanimous decision even went so far as to declare that providing a computer intermediary did not make the claims patentable since the steps performed by the computer were ordinary. In other words, simply "computerizing" a conventional process is not patentable.

Statutory Classes: Machines

Machines are devices or things used for accomplishing a task. Like processes, they usually involve some activity or motion performed by working parts, but in machines, the emphasis is on the parts or hardware rather than the activity. Another way of saying this is that a process involves the actual steps of manipulation, while a machine is a thing that does the manipulating. That said, many inventions can be claimed as a process or as a machine. For instance, a new type of weaving machine can be claimed in terms of its actual hardware or as a process for weaving fabrics, provided the weaving process is novel. Examples of conventional machines include cigarette lighters, robots, sewage treatment plants, clocks, electronic circuits, automobiles, boats, rockets, TVs, computers, printers, lasers, and photocopiers.

Software inventions can also be claimed as machines. Whether the software invention is categorized as a process or machine, or both, depends on how the invention is described in the patent application's claims section.

If possible, both types of claims should usually be provided in a single patent application. This difference in the claims is a simple change of language. The example below involves a software invention that controls a milling machine.

EXAMPLE: A system for controlling a milling machine can be claimed either as a process or a machine. As a process, the system would be claimed as follows:

1. A process for controlling a milling machine, comprising:
   a. measuring an object to obtain a set of measurements, and
   b. controlling a milling machine according to the set of measurements.

As a machine, the system would be claimed as follows:

2. An apparatus for controlling a milling machine, comprising:
   a. means [or an apparatus] for measuring an object to obtain a set of measurements, and
   b. means [or an apparatus] for adjusting a milling machine according to the set of measurements.

Note that the first step or means for measuring can be regarded as either an action or the hardware for performing the action. This applies equally to the second step.

Statutory Classes: Manufactures

Manufactures, sometimes termed "articles of manufacture," are elementary items made by human hands or machines. Most manufactures have few or no working or moving parts as prime features. Examples are erasers, desks, houses, wires, tires, books, cloth, chairs, containers, transistors, dolls, hairpieces, ladders, envelopes, buildings, floppy disks, knives, hand tools, and boxes.

There is some overlap between the machine and the manufacture categories. Many devices, such as mechanical pencils, cigarette lighters, and electronic circuits, can be classified as either.

Manufactures do not include naturally occurring things, like rocks, gold, shrimp, or wood, or slightly modified naturally occurring things, like a shrimp with its head and vein removed. However, suppose an inventor discovers a new and nonobvious use for a naturally occurring thing, such as using the molecules in a piece of gold as part of computer memory. In that case, this invention can be patented as a new use (see below) or as a machine.

Statutory Classes: Compositions of Matter

Compositions of matter are chemical compositions, conglomerates, aggregates, or other chemically significant substances usually supplied in bulk (solid or particulate), liquid, or gaseous form. Examples are road-building compositions, chemicals, gasoline, fuel gas, glue, paper, soap, drugs, microbes, food additives, and plastics.

Although naturally occurring things such as wood and rocks can't be patented, purified forms of naturally occurring things, such as medicinals extracted from herbs, can be. One inventor obtained a composition of matter patent on a new element he discovered. Recently, genetically altered plants, microbes, and nonhuman animals have been allowed under this category. Compositions sometimes overlap with manufactures. Unlike manufactures, compositions are usually similar chemical compositions or aggregates whose chemical natures are of primary importance and whose shapes are of secondary import. Manufactures are items whose physical shapes are significant but whose chemical compositions are of lesser import.

Examples of Inventions That Don't Fit Within a Statutory Class

- Processes performed solely with one's mind (such as a meditation method or a speed-reading method) do not involve novel body actions.
- Naturally occurring phenomena and articles, even if modified somewhat.
- Laws of nature, including abstract scientific or mathematical principles. (John Napier's invention of logarithms in 1614 was immensely innovative and valuable, but today it would never get past the bottom level statutory class of the patentability steps.)
- An arrangement of printed matter without some accompanying instrumentality. Printed matter by itself isn't patentable, but a printed label on a mattress telling how to turn it to ensure even wear or dictionary index tabs that guide a reader to the desired word more rapidly have been patented as articles of manufacture.
  - Methods or computer programs that have no practical utility, that is, that don't produce any commercially useful and tangible result. Thus, an algorithm for solving π to 15 decimal places or extracting square roots would not be in a statutory class. While securities trading systems, credit accounting systems, etc., involving an account and file postings, have been held patentable, the validity of these patents is now in doubt because of the *Alice* decision discussed above.
- Ideas. Thoughts or goals not expressed in concrete form or use are not assignable to any of the five categories above. An inventor must show how an idea can be made and used to be useful in a tangible form. Even if this expression is only on paper, the PTO will accept it.
- Certain processes. Processes that are either not tied to a particular machine or apparatus or that do not transform an article into a different state or thing.

New Uses of Any of the Above

In addition to the four statutory classes discussed above, an inventor who discovers a new and nonobvious use of an old invention or thing can get a patent on the discovery. For example, suppose an inventor discovers that a Venetian-blind cleaning device can also be used as a seed planter. The inventor can't get a patent on the physical hardware that constitutes the Venetian-blind cleaning device because the inventor didn't create it—someone already patented, invented, or designed it first—but an inventor can get a patent on the specific new use (seed planting). For example, one inventor obtained a patent on a new use for aspirin: feeding it to swine to increase their growth rate, and one got a patent on the new use of a powerful vacuum to suck prairie dogs out of the ground.

New-use inventions are relatively rare and technically are a form of, and must be claimed as, a process. (35 U.S.C. § 100(b).)

Utility

To be patentable, an invention must be useful. Patent applications are rarely rejected for lack of utility. Any usefulness will suffice, provided the usefulness is functional and not aesthetic. However, utility is occasionally an issue when an inventor tries to patent a new chemical for which a use hasn't yet been found. Its inventor will likely find a use later. If the inventor can't state (and prove, if challenged) a realistic use, the PTO won't grant a patent on the chemical. A chemical that can be used to produce another useful chemical is itself regarded as useful.

Commercially sold software-based inventions almost always satisfy the utility requirement because virtually all software has a useful function, even if used to create aesthetic designs on an idle monitor, compute the value of mutual funds, or evaluate golf scores.

Even though virtually all inventions are useful in the literal sense of the word, some types of inventions are deemed "not useful" as a matter of law, and the PTO accordingly denies patents on them. Below are some examples:

- **Unsafe new drugs.** The PTO won't grant a patent on any new drug unless the applicant can show that it is useful in treating some condition and that it's relatively safe for its intended purpose. In other words, the PTO considers an unsafe drug useless. Most drug patent applications won't be allowed unless the Food and Drug Administration (FDA) has approved tests of the drug for efficacy and safety. Drugs that are generally recognized as safe, or are in a "safe" chemical category with known safe drugs, don't need prior FDA approval to be patentable.

- **Whimsical inventions.** On rare occasions, the PTO will reject a patent application when it finds the invention to be whimsical, even though "useful" in some bizarre sense. This standard is rarely applied. For example, in 1937, the PTO issued a patent on a rear windshield (with tail-operated wiper) for a horse (Pat. No. 2,079,053). The PTO regarded this as having utility as an amusement.

- **Inventions useful only for illegal purposes.** The PTO won't issue patents on inventions useful solely for illegal purposes such as disabling burglar alarms, safecracking, copying currency, and defrauding the public. However, many inventions in this category can be described or claimed in a "legal" way. For example, a police radar detector would qualify for a patent if described as a tester to see if a radar is working or as a device for reminding drivers to watch their speed.

- **Immoral inventions.** In the past, the PTO has included morality in its requirements, rejecting inventions believed to be morally objectionable. In recent years, with increased sexual liberality, the requirement is now virtually nonexistent. The PTO now regularly issues patents on sexual aids and stimulants.

- **Nonoperable inventions.** Another facet of the useful requirement is operability. The invention must appear to the PTO to be workable. The PTO will reject as nonoperable an esoteric invention that looks technically questionable (in other words, it looks like it just plain won't work). If the examiner questions operability—a rare occurrence—the inventor has the burden of proving its operability. Any inventor whose claims are rejected for inoperability has the right to bring a working prototype to the PTO to demonstrate its operability. While all patent examiners have technical degrees and can apply a very stringent test if the operability of an invention is questioned, in several cases, examiners have dropped their guard and allowed patents for perpetual motion or perpetual energy machines to issue.
- **Nuclear weapons.** Nuclear weapons aren't patentable because of a particular statute.
- **Theoretical phenomena.** Theoretical phenomena, such as the phenomenon of superconductivity or the transistor effect, aren't patentable. However, hardware, or a process involving hardware that uses a new theoretical phenomenon, is considered useful.
- **Aesthetic purpose.** If the invention's sole purpose or "function" is aesthetic, the PTO will reject it as lacking utility. These inventions should usually be the subject of a design patent application. For example, consider a computer case whose unique shape does not make the computer operate better. If the only novelty is the design's aesthetics, the case could be covered by a design patent. If the computer case's shape made it cheaper to manufacture, it has utility and could be covered by a utility patent.

Novelty and Prior Art

The criteria for novelty has not changed dramatically since the 19th century. Still, before examining this standard, it is necessary to review prior art subject (In Chapter 4, we discuss how to search for prior art.)

Prior Art

An invention must be novel to qualify for a patent. For an invention to meet this novelty test, it must differ physically in some way from all prior developments available to the public anywhere in the world. In the realm of patent law, these prior developments and concepts are collectively referred to as "prior art." The PTO will not grant a patent if the prior art shows that an invention already exists and will cancel an existing registration if prior art is discovered after a patent has been issued. Because an invention must not already exist to receive patent protection, a patent applicant must often overcome prior-art objections by showing how the claimed invention differs from the prior art.

Prior art consists of:

- any published writing (including any patent) by another, not acting for the inventor, that was made publicly available any time before the effective filing date
- any U.S. patent whose filing or issue date is before the effective filing date
- any relevant invention or development by another not acting for the inventor (whether described in writing or not) existing before the effective filing date, or
- any public or commercial use, sale, or knowledge of the invention (no matter who made it) more than one year before the effective filing date.

Year Date Format

The year-month-day date format (2021 June 10) used in this book is from the International Standards Organization (ISO). It is commonly used in computer-speak, in the PTO's electronic filing system, and trademark applications. It provides a logical descending order that facilitates calculating the one-year rule and other periods.

The Effective Filing Date

The patent application's effective filing date is usually the actual filing date of a regular utility patent application (also known as a "nonprovisional" application). Suppose before filing the regular application, the inventor has filed a corresponding earlier patent application in another country or jurisdiction with a treaty with the United States. In that case, the foreign filing date is the effective date provided that the foreign application discloses how to make and use the invention. It must be referenced in the regular U.S. application to obtain the "priority" of the earlier foreign application.

Alternatively, an applicant may file a provisional patent application (PPA). This is a simple interim application that provides an earlier filing date.) Like a foreign application, the PPA discloses how to make and use the invention, and it must be referenced in the regular application.

Suppose the claimed invention was made available to the public from any source other than the inventor before the present application's effective filing date. In that case, such availability is valid as prior art. But if the invention was made available to the public by the inventor within the year before the invention's effective filing date, this availability is not considered valid prior art.

Prior Use Defense

Suppose your patent covers an invention that is a process or a machine, manufacture, or composition of matter used in a manufacturing or other commercial process. And suppose you find an infringer who had used the invention in the United States commercially, more than one year before either (a) your patent's filing date, or (b) the date you disclosed the invention to the public. In any of these cases, the alleged infringer has a complete defense to any claim of infringement of your patent.

The One-Year Rule

A U.S. inventor has one year to file a patent application after the inventor, or someone acting for the inventor, sells, offers for sale, or commercially or publicly uses or describes the invention. If an inventor fails to file within one year of such occurrence, the inventor is barred from obtaining a patent. If the PTO is unaware of the public sale or use and issues a patent, that patent can be declared invalid if it can later be shown that the invention was publicly shown or sold by the inventor or the inventor's cohorts more than one year before filing.

Foreign Filing and the One-Year Rule

While an inventor has a year to file in the United States after the inventor publishes or uses the invention, most foreign countries aren't so lenient. Suppose an inventor intends to file a foreign patent application. In that case, the invention should not be offered for sale, sold, publicly used, or published anywhere before the inventor files in the United States.

For instance, suppose an inventor creates a new type of paint roller on 2020 November 17. Suppose the inventor has no intention of filing in another country. In that case, the inventor or the inventor's associates can use, publish, or sell the invention immediately and still file the U.S. patent application (PPA or regular/nonprovisional) any time up to 2021, November 17.

However, any inventor who may eventually want to file a foreign application should file in the United States before publicizing the invention. This way, the inventor can publish or sell the invention freely without losing any foreign rights in the major industrial countries, provided the inventor files there within one year after the U.S. filing date.

Under an international agreement, the inventor is entitled to the U.S. filing date in such countries. In countries that are not a party to any patent treaties (for example, Colombia and Pakistan), the inventor must file before publicizing the invention. (For more information about foreign patents, see Chapter 9.)

The Public Doesn't Have to Access "Publicly Accessible" Prior Art

The CAFC held that a prior-art reference was valid regardless of whether the patent owner accessed the reference. What mattered was whether the prior art was "publicly accessible." To be publicly accessible, a person of ordinary skill in the art could, through the exercise of reasonable diligence, access the reference. (*Samsung Elecs. Co., Ltd. v. Infobridge PTE. Ltd.*, Nos. 2018-2007, 2018-2012, 2019 U.S. App. LEXIS 20678 (Fed. Cir. July 12, 2019).)

Specifics of Prior Art

Let's take a closer look at the definition of prior art. (35 U.S.C. § 102.)

Prior Printed Publications Anywhere

Prior art includes any printed publication, written by anyone, and from anywhere in the world, in any language. Prior art can be used to reject the claims of a patent application if it was published either: (a) up to one year before the application's effective filing date (see above) and did not come from the inventor or anyone acting on behalf of the inventor, or (b) more than one year before the application's effective filing date, even if it came from the inventor or someone acting for the inventor.

The term "printed publication" is broadly interpreted, and the PTO has even used old Dick Tracy comic strips showing a wristwatch radio as prior art. Generally, printed publications include patents (U.S. and foreign), books, magazines (including trade and professional journals), publicly available technical papers and abstracts, and even photocopied theses, provided they were made publicly available by putting them in a college library. While the statute speaks of "printed" publications, we believe that information that is publicly accessible on a computer information utility or network would be considered a printed publication.

U.S. Patents Filed by Others

Any U.S. patent that has a filing date earlier than an inventor's effective filing date is considered valid prior art. This is so even if the patent issues after an inventor files an application.

It is a common misconception that only in-force patents (that is, patents that haven't yet expired) count as prior art. Even if it were issued 150 years ago, any earlier patent would constitute prior art against an invention. (For information about how to search for patents, see Chapter 4.)

Publicly Available Knowledge in the United States

Prior art is valid even if there's no written record of it. Any public knowledge of the invention will constitute valid prior art. Likewise, the use of the invention by the inventor (or others in the United States) before the inventor's earliest provable date of invention, or one year before the inventor files a patent application, will constitute valid prior art.

> **EXAMPLE:** An inventor invents a new type of paint and uses it to paint his building in downtown Philadelphia. The inventor forgets to file a patent application and leaves the paint on for 13 months. It's now too late to file a valid patent application because the invention was used publicly for more than a year.

Other examples of prior public knowledge include an earlier heat-treating process used openly by a blacksmith in a small town (although never published or widely known), a talk at a publicly accessible technical society, and the showing of a kaleidoscope without restriction at a party with 30 attendees.

The PTO rarely uses this public-use-and-knowledge category of the prior art because they have no way of uncovering it. The PTO searches only patents and other publications. Occasionally, however, if defendants (infringers) in patent lawsuits happen to uncover a prior public use, they can then rely on it to invalidate the patent and escape infringement liability.

EXAMPLE: A 3M employee developed a method for perforating carbon-less paper with a laser and arranged to manufacture 10,000 forms using the laser-perforated sheets. In July 1989, the laser-perforated forms were distributed throughout the company for use by thousands of 3M employees. 3M filed a patent application for its laser-perforation method in August 1990. After 3M acquired a patent, 3M sued Appleton Papers for infringement of the process. As a defense, Appleton claimed that the patent was invalid because 3M put the invention "in public use" more than one year before its patent application date. A federal court determined that the internal distribution at 3M constituted a public use, and the patent was declared invalid. (*3M v. Appleton Papers Inc.*, 35 F.Supp.2d 1138 (D. Minn., 1999).)

Experimental Exception

If a prior public use was for bona fide (good-faith) experimental purposes, it doesn't count as prior art. For example, suppose in the "painted Philadelphia building" example above that an inventor painted his building to test the new paint's durability: Each month, the inventor photographed it, kept records on its reflectivity, wear resistance, and adhesion. In this case, the one-year period wouldn't begin to run until the bona fide experimentation stopped.

An Inventor's Prior Foreign Patents

If an inventor (or the inventor's legal representative) obtains any foreign patent before the inventor's U.S. filing date and the foreign patent application was filed more than a year before the U.S. filing date, it is valid prior art. This category is generally pertinent to non-U.S. residents who start the patenting process in a foreign country. An inventor in this class must file the U.S. application either within one year after filing in a foreign country or before the foreign patent issues. However, an inventor seeking the benefit of a foreign filing date for a U.S. application should file in the United States within one year after the foreign filing date.

Prior U.S. Inventor

Suppose someone (the first inventor) in the United States filed a patent application with an effective filing date before another inventor's effective filing date (the second inventor). In that case, the first inventor's filing could defeat a right to a patent for the second inventor. However, under an exception, if an invention is novel and the first inventor worked in the same organization as the second inventor, then the first inventor's work won't be considered prior art.

Prior Sale or On-Sale Status in the United States

Suppose an inventor offers to sell, sells, or commercially uses an invention in the United States. The inventor must file the U.S. patent application within one year after this offer, sale, or commercial use.

To start the one year running, the sale or offer of sale must be a commercial offer to sell or a sale of actual hardware or a process embodying the invention. This is true even if the invention has not yet been built, so long as it has been drawn or described in reasonable detail. However, an offer to license or sell, or an actual sale of the inventive concept (not hardware) to a manufacturer, will not start the one year running. (If the sale or offer to sell was not made by the inventor or someone acting on the inventor's behalf, then the one-year rule does not apply, and any such sale or offer will defeat the inventor's right to a patent, even if made one day before the inventor files the patent application.)

What about secret sales? The Supreme Court ruled that the sale of an invention to a third party who is obligated to keep the invention secret places the invention "on-sale." This bars a person from receiving a patent on an invention that was "in public use, on sale, or otherwise available to the public before the effective filing date of the claimed invention." (35 U.S.C. § 102(a)(1).) In other words, like prior law, an inventor's "secret sale" of an invention to a third party qualifies as prior art for purposes of determining patent eligibility. (*Helsinn Healthcare S.A. v. Teva Pharmaceuticals USA, Inc.* 139 S. Ct. 628 (2019).)

Abandonment

If an inventor "abandons" an invention by finally giving up on it, and this comes to the attention of the PTO or any court, the application will be rejected, or the patent ruled invalid.

EXAMPLE: An inventor made a model of an invention, tested it, failed to get it to work, or failed to sell it, and then consciously dropped all efforts on it. Later the inventor changes her mind and tries to patent it. If the abandonment becomes known, the inventor will lose the right to a patent. But if the inventor merely stops work on it for several years because of such reasons as health, finances, or lack of a crucial part, but intends to pursue it again when possible, the law would excuse the inaction and hold that the inventor didn't abandon.

Novelty: What Is "New"?

The law generally recognizes three types of novelty, any one of which will satisfy the novelty requirement: (1) a physical (hardware or method) difference, (2) a new combination or rearrangement, and (3) new use of old hardware.

Physical Difference

An invention must have some physical or structural (hardware or method) difference over the prior art. If the invention is a machine, composition, or article, it must have one or more parts with a different shape, value, size, color, or composition than what's already known.

It's often difficult for inventors to distinguish between a physical difference and a new result. When asked, "What's physically different about the invention?" inventors often reply that it is lighter, faster, safer, cheaper to make or use, or portable. However, these factors are new results or advantages, not physical differences, and are primarily relevant to nonobviousness, not novelty. A new physical feature must be a difference in the hardware.

Even omitting an element can be considered novel. For example, if a machine has always had four gears, and an inventor finds that it will work with three, the novelty requirement is satisfied.

Also, the discovery of a critical area of a given prior-art range will be considered novel. That is, if a prior-art magazine article on fabric dyeing states that a substance will work at a temperature range of 100–150 degrees centigrade and an inventor discovers that it works five times better at 127–130 degrees centigrade, the law will still consider this range novel even though the prior art technically embraces it.

One area of novelty that is frequently overlooked is the new arrangement: If an inventor comes up with a new arrangement of an old combination of elements, the new arrangement will satisfy the novelty requirement.

A physical difference can also be subtle or less apparent in the hardware sense so that it's manifested primarily by a different mode of operation. For example, an electronic amplifying circuit that looks the same, but that operates in a different mode—say Class A rather than Class B—or is under the control of different software, or a pump that looks the same, but that operates at a higher pressure and hence in a different mode, will be considered novel.

Processes Note

If an invention is a new process, novel hardware is unnecessary; the physical novelty is the new way of manipulating old hardware. Any novel step or steps will satisfy the physical novelty requirement.

New Combination

Many laypersons believe that if an invention consists entirely of old components, it can't be patented. This is not true. Most inventions are made of old components. If an invention is a new combination or rearrangement of two old features, the PTO will consider it novel. For a combination invention to be considered as lacking novelty, all of its physical characteristics must exist in a single prior-art reference. For example, suppose an inventor "invents" a bicycle made of one of the recently discovered, superstrength, carbon- fiber alloys. The bicycle would be considered novel because it has a new physical feature: a frame that is made, for the first time, of a carbon-fiber alloy. Remember, just because it's novel, useful, and fits within a statutory class, doesn't mean the bicycle is patentable. It still must pass the test of nonobviousness.

New Use

If you've invented a new use for an old item of hardware or an old process, the new use will satisfy the novelty requirement no matter how trivial the "newness." For example, Dorie invents a new vegetable cooker that, after a search, she discovers is precisely like a copper smelter invented by one Jaschik in 1830. Even though identical to Jaschik's smelter, Dorie's cooker will be considered novel because it's for a different use. However, technically, if an invention involves novel physical hardware, it can't be a new-use invention.

Nonobviousness

Even though an invention is physically different from the prior art, this isn't enough to qualify for a patent. To obtain a patent, the differences must be significant. The legal term for such a difference is "unobvious" or, commonly, "nonobvious." To obtain a patent, the differences between the invention and the prior art must not be obvious to one with ordinary skill in the field. As it is sometimes put, the invention must provide one or more new and unexpected results.

In the following sections, we discuss examples of "nonobviousness" and "obviousness." We also cover the types of arguments based on external circumstances (called "secondary factors") that are often made to bolster an inventor's contention that an invention is nonobvious.

A patentability flowchart is provided below as Figure 2B to help you understand the slippery concept of nonobviousness and its role in the patent application process. In addition to presenting the PTO and the courts' criteria for determining whether an invention is nonobvious, the chart also incorporates the first three tests of statutory class, usefulness, and novelty.

Nonobviousness Determination Can Be Based on Common Sense

In a 2009 case, a court invalidated a patent for an email distribution system. The patent claimed a method for managing bulk email distribution to groups of consumers, including selecting recipients, sending emails to that group, and tabulating the number of emails transmitted successfully. If the number did not exceed a certain minimum, the last step called for repeating the previous steps. The court summarized the last step as obvious since it was based on the commonsense principle, "If at first, you don't succeed, try again." (*Perfect Web Technologies, Inc. v. InfoUSA, Inc.*, 587 F.3d 1324 (Fed. Cir. 2009).)

How Patent Examiners Determine "Nonobviousness"

Patent examiners first search and gather all of the patents and other prior art they feel are relevant or close to the invention for which a patent is sought. Then they examine these patents and any prior-art references provided with the patent application and see whether the invention contains any novel physical features, new combinations, or new uses that aren't shown in any reference. If so, an invention is novel.

Next, they see whether the novelty produces any unexpected or surprising results. If so, they'll find that the invention is nonobvious and grant an inventor a patent. If not (this usually occurs the first time they act on a case), they'll reject the application (sometimes termed a "shotgun"

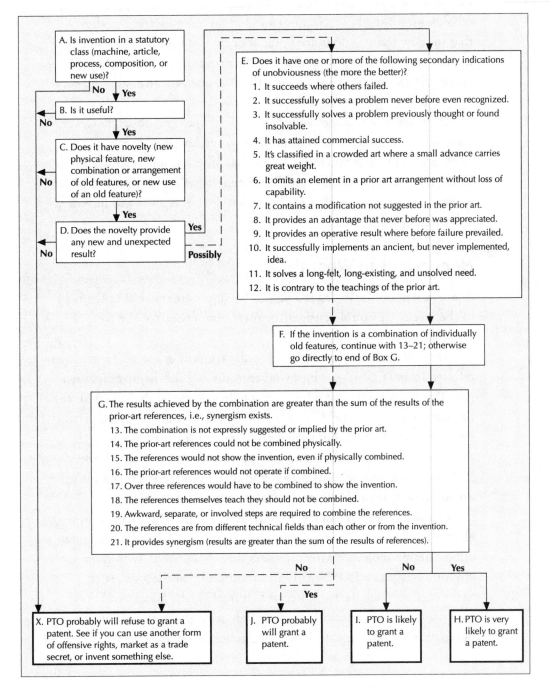

Figure 2B—The Patentability Flowchart

or "shoot-from-the-hip" rejection) and leave it to an inventor to show that the new features do indeed produce new and unexpected results. To do this, an inventor may use many of the relevant reasons listed in this chapter. If an inventor can convince the examiner, the inventor will get the patent.

If a dispute over nonobviousness finds its way into court, however, both sides will present the testimony of patent lawyers or technical experts who fit, or most closely fit, the hypothetical job descriptions called for by the particular case. These experts will testify for or against obviousness by arguing that the invention does or doesn't produce new and unexpected results.

Nonobvious to Whom?

A patent will not be issued if a person having ordinary skill in the field of the invention would consider the invention obvious at the time of creation.

The law considers a person with ordinary skill in the art (sometimes referred to as POSITA) to be a worker in the field of the invention who has (1) ordinary skill, but who (2) is totally knowledgeable about all the prior art in his or her field. This is pure fantasy because no such person ever lived, or ever will, but there's no other realistic way to approach an objective standard for determining nonobviousness. Instead, the PTO creates a hypothetical person and tries to weigh the invention's obviousness against this hypothetical person's knowledge.

Consider some examples. Assume that an invention has to do with electronics—say, a new computer circuit process. A typical computer circuit design engineer with complete knowledge of all computer circuits satisfy as a POSITA. If an invention is mechanical, such as an improved cigarette lighter or belt buckle, the PTO would try to postulate a hypothetical cigarette lighter engineer or belt buckle designer with ordinary skill and comprehensive knowledge.

What Does "Obvious" Mean?

So many commonplace inventions, such as bifocals and paper clips, seem obvious to us now but were quite revolutionary in their time. Over the years, many tests for nonobviousness have been used by the courts. One crucial decision stated that nonobviousness is manifested if the invention produces "unusual and surprising results." The U.S. Supreme Court, which has the final say in such matters, decreed the steps for determining nonobviousness in the case of *Graham v. John Deere*. Here they are:

1. Determine the scope and content of the prior art.
2. Determine the novelty of the invention.
3. Determine the level of skill of artisans in the pertinent art.
4. Against this background, determine the obviousness or nonobviousness of the inventive subject matter.
5. Also, consider secondary and objective factors, such as commercial success, long-felt but unsolved need, and others' failure. (*Graham v. John Deere*, 383 U.S. 1 (1966).)

Despite its failure to define the term "obvious" in the crucial step 4, the Supreme Court did add an essential step to the process by which obviousness is to be determined. In Step 5, the Court made clear that objective circumstances must be taken into account by the PTO or courts when deciding whether an invention is or isn't obvious. The Court specifically mentioned three such circumstances: commercial success, long-felt but unsolved need, and others' failure to come up with the invention.

Although an invention might not, strictly speaking, produce "new and unexpected results" from the standpoint of one with "ordinary skill in the art," it still may be considered nonobvious if it can be shown that the invention has met some of these secondary factors.

Determining Nonobviousness

In the following sections, we describe circumstances that can affect the determination of nonobviousness.

Slight Physical Changes—Dramatic Result

Usually, an invention must demonstrate a significant physical change to be considered nonobvious. However, on some occasions, a very slight change in the shape, slope, size, or material can produce a patentable invention that operates entirely differently and produces unexpected results.

> EXAMPLE: Consider the original centrifugal vegetable juicer composed of a spinning perforated basket with a vertical sidewall and a nonperforated grater bottom. When vegetables, such as carrots, were pushed into the grater bottom, they were grated into fine pieces and juice thrown against the basket's sidewall. The juice passed through the perforations and was recovered in a container. Still, the pieces clung to the sidewalls, adding weight to the basket and closing the perforations, making the machine impossible to run and operate after a relatively small amount of vegetables were juiced. Then someone discovered that making the side of the basket slope outward still allowed the juice to be extracted through the basket's perforated side. Still, now the pulp, instead of adhering to the old vertical side of the basket, was centrifugally forced up the new sloped side of the basket where it would go over the top and be diverted to a separate receptacle. Thus the juicer could be operated continuously without the pulp having to be cleaned out. Although the physical novelty was slight and involved merely changing the slope of a basket's sidewall, the result was entirely new and unexpected. It was, therefore, considered nonobvious.

New-Use Inventions

New-use inventions don't involve any physical change at all in the old invention. However, to be considered nonobvious, the new use must be (1) a different use of some known product or process, and (2) the different use must produce new, unexpected results.

> **EXAMPLE:** One inventor found that feeding aspirin to swine increased their rate of growth. This discovery was considered nonobvious because the result—faster-growing swine—was unexpected because it wasn't described or suggested in the prior art.

When Is a Combination Invention Obvious?

In a 2007 case, *KSR v. Teleflex*, the U.S. Supreme Court made it easier for the PTO or the courts to reject claims or hold patents invalid if those patents are based on a combination of references. Teleflex owned a patent that combined two well-known components—a gas pedal that can be adjusted relative to the driver's seating position and an electronic (as opposed to a mechanical) sensor that senses and transmits to the vehicle's throttle computer the position of the pedal. Teleflex sued its competitor, KSR International, of Canada, for supplying General Motors with adjustable gas pedals with their sensors for use with electronic throttle controls. The Supreme Court decided that when elements, techniques, items, or devices are combined, united, or arranged, the resulting combination—something the Court called "ordinary innovation"—is not patentable. Therefore, ordinary engineering that engineers perform in their usual day-to-day activities may not be patentable. Before this, the case law held that an invention should not be held obvious over several prior-art references unless there is a suggestion, motivation, or teaching that the references can or should be combined. KSR held that there must be some apparent reason in the prior art to justify combining the references—for example, the existence of a problem can make it obvious to try various solutions. (*KSR v. Teleflex*, 550 U.S. 398 (2007).)

Different Element, Similar Function

The courts have held that the substitution of a different, but similarly functioning, element for one of the elements in a known combination, although creating a "novel" invention, won't produce a nonobvious one. For example, many companies in the 1950s substituted transistors for vacuum tubes in amplifier circuits. This new combination of old elements provided tremendous new results (decreased power consumption, size, heat, weight, and far greater longevity), but it wasn't patentable because the results were foreseeable. The power reduction and reduced-weight advantages of transistors would have been already known as soon as a transistor made its appearance. Thus, substituting them for tubes wouldn't provide the old amplifier circuit with any unexpected new results. Accordingly, the PTO's Board of Appeals held the new combination to be obvious to an artisan of ordinary skill at the time.

Old Concept, New Form

The PTO will also consider as obvious the mere carrying forward of an old concept, or a change in form and degree, without a new result.

For instance, when one inventor provided notches on the steering wheel's inner rim to provide a better grip, the idea was held to be obvious because of medieval sword handles that had similar notches for the same purpose. And the use of a large pulley for a logging rig was held nonpatentable over the use of a small pulley for clotheslines. These cases are known as "obviousness by analogy."

> EXAMPLE: Lou comes up with a way to make mustard-flavored hot dog buns—mix powdered mustard with the flour. Even though Lou's recipe is novel, the PTO will almost certainly hold it obvious because the result of the new combination is entirely foreseeable and expected.

There is an exception to this rule. If the substitution provides unexpected new results, the law will hold it nonobvious.

Duplication of Parts

The courts and the PTO will usually consider the duplication of a part as obvious unless new results can be observed. For instance, in an automobile, the substitution of two banks of three cylinders with two carburetors was held obvious over a six-cylinder, single-carburetor engine because the new arrangement had no unexpected advantages. However, there are exceptions to this rule. For example, the use of two water turbines to provide cross-flow to eliminate axial thrust on bearings was held nonobvious over a single turbine; again, an unexpected, new result.

Portability, Size, Speed, and Integration

Making devices portable, making parts smaller or larger, faster or slower, effecting a substitution of equivalents (a roller bearing for a ball bearing), making elements adjustable, making parts integral, separable (modular), or in kit form, and other known techniques with their known advantages, will be held obvious unless new, unexpected results can be shown.

Secondary Factors in Determining Nonobviousness

Suppose the new and unexpected results of an invention are marginal. In that case, an inventor may still get a patent if the invention possesses one or more secondary factors that establish nonobviousness. While the Supreme Court listed only three in the *John Deere* case, we have compiled a list of factors that the PTO and the courts consider.

These secondary factors must generally be dealt with only if the PTO makes a preliminary finding of obviousness or if an invention is attacked in court as being obvious. Although some of these secondary factors may appear similar, consider each independently because the courts have recognized subtle differences:

- **Previous failure of others.** If the invention is successful where previous workers in the field were unable to make it work, this will significantly help the application. For instance, many previous attempts were made to use electrostatic methods for making photocopies, but all failed. Chester Carlson (a patent attorney himself) came along and successfully used an electrostatic process to make copies. This greatly enhanced his case for the patentability of his dry (xerographic) photocopying process.

- **Solves an unrecognized problem.** Some inventions solve problems that are not obvious. Consider a showerhead that automatically shuts off in case of extreme water temperature. As the problem was likely never recognized in the prior art, the solution would probably be nonobvious.

- **Solves an insoluble problem.** Suppose that for years those skilled in the art had tried and failed to solve a problem and the art and literature were full of unsuccessful "solutions." Nonobviousness may be demonstrated if an inventor finds a workable solution, for example, a cure for the common cold.

- **Commercial success.** If an invention has attained commercial success, this helps to prove nonobviousness. After all, nothing succeeds like success, right? However, this argument is not always available because many inventors don't sell the invention before the application is filed, either because of concern over foreign patent rights or the one-year rule.

- **Crowded art.** If an invention is in a crowded field of invention — for example, a field that is mature and that contains many patents, such as electrical connectors or bicycles—a small advance will go further towards qualifying the invention for a patent than it will in a new, blossoming field of invention.

- **Omission of element.** Suppose an inventor can omit an element in a prior invention without loss of capability. In that case, this will count a lot toward proving nonobviousness because parts are often expensive, unreliable, heavy, and labor-intensive.

- **Unsuggested modification.** Suppose an inventor can modify a prior invention in a manner not suggested before, such as increasing the slope in a paper-making machine or making the basket slope in a centrifugal juice extractor. In that case, this act in itself counts for nonobviousness.

- **Unappreciated advantage.** If an invention provides an advantage that was never before appreciated, it can make a difference. In a recent case, a gas cap that was impossible to insert in a skewed manner was patentable because it provided an advantage that was never previously appreciated.

- **Solves prior inoperability.** If an invention provides an operative result where before only inoperability existed, then it has a good chance for a patent. For instance, nonobviousness would be proved if an inventor came up with a gasoline additive that prevented massive fires in case of a plane crash because all previous fire-suppressant additives had been largely unsuccessful.

- **Successful implementation of ancient idea.** Consider the Wright Brothers' airplane. For centuries humans had wanted to fly and had tried many unsuccessful schemes. The successful implementation of such an ancient desire carries significant weight when it comes to proving nonobviousness.

- **Solution of long-felt need.** Suppose an inventor finds a way to prevent tailgate-type automobile crashes. This solves a powerful need, and the solution will help demonstrate nonobviousness.

- **Contrary to prior art's teaching.** If the prior art expressly teaches that something can't be done or is impractical—for example, humans can't fly without artificial propulsion motors—a patent will issue if the inventor can prove this teaching wrong.

Combination Inventions: Secondary Factors

Inventions that combine two or more elements already known in the prior art can still be patentable provided the combination can be considered nonobvious. That is, it's a new combination, and it produces new and unexpected results. Most patents are granted on such combinations because very few genuinely new things are ever discovered.

Below are some of the factors used to determine the nonobviousness of "combination inventions" (that is, inventions that have two or more features that are shown in two or more prior-art references):

- **Synergism (2 + 2 = 5).** If the results achieved by a combination invention are greater than the sum of its parts' results, this can indicate nonobviousness. Consider a pistol trigger release where a magnetic ring must be worn to fire the pistol. The results (increased police safety) are far more than what magnets, rings, and pistols could provide separately.

- **Combination unsuggested.** If the prior art contains no suggestion, either expressed or implied, that the references should be combined, this weighs in favor of nonobviousness.

- **Impossible to combine.** If the prior-art references show the separate elements of the inventive combination, but in a way that makes it seem they would be physically impossible to combine, this can demonstrate nonobviousness.

- **Different combination.** An inventor has a good case for nonobviousness if the prior art for the combination of elements shows a different, albeit possibly confusingly similar, combination of the inventor's result.

- **Prior-art references would not operate in combination.** An inventor also has a good case for nonobviousness if prior-art references indicate that the combination of elements wouldn't operate properly, for example, due to some incompatibility. If an inventor found a way to make that combination work, this would favor nonobviousness.

- **References from a different field.** If the prior-art references show similar structures to an invention, this helps demonstrate nonobviousness in a different technical field.

Additional arguments can be made to demonstrate nonobviousness, much of which are beyond this book's scope. For additional information, review some of the patent resources provided in Chapter 10.

Design Patent Requirements

Whereas a utility patent covers an invention whose novel feature(s) produces a useful result, a design patent covers an invention whose novel features produce a different aesthetic or ornamental appearance. A design must meet three requirements to qualify for a design patent. The design must be:

- new and original
- nonobvious, and
- an ornamental design for a useful article of manufacture.

Note that a design patent can be granted only if the design is embodied on an article of manufacture—a term that encompasses anything made "by the hands of man" from raw materials, whether literally by hand or by machinery or by art. (*In re Hruby*, 373 F.2d 997 (CCPA 1967).) Although the term "article of manufacture" is broad and includes everything from computer icons to wallpaper, it is not meant to include paintings, silkscreens, photographs, or separable two-dimensional surface ornamentation, such as decals. However, this distinction is difficult to pin down. For example, a roof shingle that mimics the appearance of wood shingles (and fools the eye into believing that a two-dimensional product is a three-dimensional product) is protectable despite its "separable" surface ornamentation and similarity to naturally occurring objects. (*National Presto Industries Inc. v. Dazey Corp.*, 18 U.S.P.Q. 2d 1113, 1116 (N.D. Ill. 1990), aff'd, 949 F.2d 402 (Fed. Cir. 1991).) A design can be patented even if it's only a portion of the article—for example, the shank of a drill bit.

Design Patents and Prior Art

For purposes of a design patent, the prior art includes:

- any design in public use or on sale or in a publication dated before the filing date of your design patent application, where the public use or sale or publication did not originate from the inventor

- any design in public use or on sale or in a publication more than one year before the filing date of your design patent application, where the public use or sale or publication did originate from the inventor
- anything that was made or built in the United States by another person and available to the public before the date your design application was filed
- anything that was made or built in the United States by you or on your behalf and available to the public more than one year before the date your design application was filed, or
- any work shown in a prior patent of another filed before your design patent application filing date.

The one-year rule for public disclosures originating with the inventor, described above, applies to designs and utility inventions.

New and Original

To be new (also referred to as "novelty"), a design must differ from the prior art (all previous product designs). A design must also be original, which means that it has to do more than simply imitate what already exists. A design that simulates a well-known object—for example, a paperweight replica of the Empire State Building or a natural object or animal or animal part—is not considered original. The design must be the result of "industry, effort, genius, or expense." (*Smith v. Whitman*, 148 U.S. 674, (1893).)

It's generally not considered original to depict something naturally occurring, but this standard is interpreted loosely. For example, a design patent for a model of a human baby was invalidated. (*In re Smith*, 77 F.2d 514 (CCPA 1935).) Still, the designers of a replica of female breasts on beads were granted a design patent and successfully enforced it against competitors (*Superior Merchandise v. M.G.I. Wholesale*, 52 U.S.P.Q. 2d 1935 (E.D. La. 1999).)

Nonobviousness

The PTO will reject a design patent application if the design is considered obvious by others in the field. As is true of the novelty standard, a concept can be obvious while the actual design (based on the concept) is not. For example, former vice president Spiro Agnew was depicted in caricature on a watch face. The concept of caricature was obvious, but the particular caricatured design of Spiro Agnew was not.

If you find the nonobvious standard for designs confusing, you're not alone. There aren't too many clear standards for determining when a design is obvious and when it's not, which means that individual patent examiners—and judges if someone files an infringement lawsuit—have a lot of leeway in making these decisions. There have been periodic attempts to change the design patent law, but the standard remains for now.

That said, it doesn't necessarily take great originality or craftsmanship to create a nonobvious design; sometimes, it requires only the ability to visualize things a little differently. For example, a designer can demonstrate nonobviousness by:

- using a familiar form in an unfamiliar medium—such as the use of a floral pattern as a candle holder
- making a slight change to an existing design that produces a striking visual effect—such as alternating the position of hearts on a wedding ring
- omitting a visual element commonly associated with similar designs—for example, a waterbed design that is distinguishable by the absence of visible seams on the top and sides of the mattress, or
- juxtaposing elements in a way that creates an unexpected visual statement—such as embedding a poker chip in the bottom of a shot glass.

A design will be more likely to meet the "nonobvious" test if one of the following is true:

- It has enjoyed commercial success.
- It has an unexpected visual appearance.
- Others have copied the design.
- Others have praised the design in the field.
- Others have tried but failed to achieve the same result.
- A design is created that others said could not be done.

Like utility inventions, a design can be novel but not obvious. For example, a court determined that a design for an alcohol server shaped like an intravenous dispenser was new—no such design had been used to serve alcohol. Still, it was obvious and therefore not patentable. (*Neo-Art, Inc. v. Hawkeye Distilled Products Co.*, 654 F.Supp. 90 (C.D. Cal. 1987), aff'd, 12 U.S.P.Q. 1572 (CAFC 1989).)

For purposes of a design patent, the difference between novelty and nonobviousness is this: A design is novel if no one has previously made a similar design. In contrast, a design is nonobvious if no one has even considered making the design. In practical terms, though, the two standards often overlap—and for design patents, lack of prior art becomes the measure of both nonobviousness and novelty.

Ornamental Design for an Article of Manufacture

For patent purposes, "design" refers to the visual and reproducible appearance of products. As the *Manual of Patent Examining Procedure* (MPEP) puts it, design "is the appearance presented by the article which creates an impression through the eye upon the mind of the observer." (MPEP § 1542.) In other words, it's the way that a product looks.

There are three common types of protectable product designs:

- shape and proportions—for example, an Eames chair
- surface ornamentation—for example, a Keith Haring Swatch watch, or
- a combination of shape and surface ornamentation—for example, an Air Jordan sports shoe.

Also, a design "must be a definite, preconceived thing, capable of reproduction and not merely the chance result of a method." (MPEP § 1502.) For example, a randomly changing laser light pattern could not be protected, but a water fountain display—the combined appearance of the water and the underlying sculpture—is protectable.

To be patentable, a design must be "primarily ornamental." This means that the article's function cannot dictate the claimed design. If a variety of designs could achieve the same function, the design is ornamental.

To be ornamental, the design should also be visible during regular intended use or at some other commercially important time—for example, at the time of sale or in an advertisement. Designs for articles that would be hidden intermittently—for example, lingerie, garment hangers, tent pegs, and inner soles for shoes—are still eligible design patents.

Plant Patents

Two types of patents can be obtained for plants: plant patents and utility patents.

Plant Patents for Plants

Since 1930, as the result of efforts by the great botanist Luther Burbank of Santa Rosa, California, the United States has been granting plant patents under the Plant Patent Act to any person who first appreciates the distinctive qualities of a plant and reproduces it asexually. Asexual reproduction means reproducing the plant by a means other than seeds, usually by grafting or cloning the plant tissue. If it cannot be duplicated by asexual reproduction, it cannot be the subject of a plant patent. The patented plant must also be novel and distinctive. Generally, this means that the plant must have at least one significant distinguishing characteristic to establish it as a distinct variety. For example, a rose may be novel and distinctive if it is nearly thornless and has a unique two-tone color scheme. Tuber-propagated plants (such as potatoes) and plants found in an uncultivated state cannot receive a plant patent. (35 U.S.C. §§ 161–164.) Similarly, the CAFC rejected two plant patent applications because the claimed oak trees (found in the wild and asexually reproduced) had not been "cultivated" as required by 35 U.S.C. § 161.

There is a limit on the extent of plant patent rights. Generally, a plant patent can only be infringed when a plant has been asexually reproduced from the actual plant protected by the plant patent. In other words, the infringing plant must have more than similar characteristics—it must have the same genetics as the patented plant.

Utility Patents for Plants

Since the late 1980s, utility patents have been issued for human-made plants or elements of plants. These plants can be reproduced either sexually (by seeds) or asexually. These patents have been issued for elements of plants such as proteins, genes, DNA, buds, pollen, fruit, plant-based chemicals, and the processes used in the manufacture of these plant products. To obtain a utility patent, the plant must be made by humans and must fit within the statutory requirements (utility, novelty, and nonobviousness). The patent must describe and claim the specific characteristics of the plant for which protection is sought. Sometimes the best way to meet this requirement is to deposit seeds or plant tissue at a specified public depository. For example, many countries have International Depository Authorities for such purposes.

Although a utility patent is more challenging and more time-consuming to acquire than a plant patent, a utility patent is considered a more potent form of protection. For example, a plant protected by a utility patent can be infringed if it is reproduced either sexually or asexually. Because the utility patent owner can prevent others from making and using the invention, does this mean the buyer of a patented seed cannot sell the resulting plants to the public? No, under patent laws, the purchaser can sell the plants but cannot manufacture the seed line.

Invention Documentation

n this chapter, we discuss documentation of inventions, an essential element in the patent process because it authenticates the conception of an invention.

The Value of Documentation

"Documentation" is the process by which the inventor records the dates and events related to the conception and reduction to practice of an invention. "Conception" is the mental part of inventing, including how an invention is formulated or how a problem is solved. "Reduction to practice" is the building and testing of the invention—that is, demonstrating that the invention works for its intended purpose. These two events and the dates upon which they occur used to be of great importance when patents were awarded to the first to invent.

> **EXAMPLE:** Years after obtaining a patent for the telephone, Alexander Graham Bell was challenged by another inventor who claimed he had first devised the telephone. Bell fought a contentious lawsuit and proved, with the aid of his lab documents and his wife's testimony, that his invention had priority. Proving how and when Bell conceived of and built his invention was crucial to his getting a patent.

After March 2013, the United States awarded patents to the first to file, not the first to invent. Although documentation remains important under current law, the outcome of Bell's telephone patent dispute might have ended differently if it occurred today. Although the dates of conception and reduction to practice are less important, we still recommend that all inventors document all steps related to the conception and development of their inventions for the reasons set forth below.

Ownership Rights

Documentation establishes who is the first and true inventor and prevents confusion over ownership rights. Documentation assists in proving ownership, for example, when two inventors simultaneously and independently conceive of an invention, or when several people are working on the same problem together. If an inventor has not filed a patent application for an invention prior to starting employment, documentation assists in proving ownership of the invention should a dispute arise with the employer.

Proof of Inventorship in Case of Dispute

Another reason that we still recommend that you continue to record your inventions as described in this chapter, is to make and retain proof that you are the true inventor and the date of your invention in case someone "derives" (a polite word for "steals") the invention from you. The PTO will enable you to institute a "derivation proceeding" that you can use to force anyone who derives the invention from you to return it to you. Similar to the former interference proceeding, you can force the turnover even if the deriver filed a patent application on the invention before you. However, you will be able to use the derivation proceeding only if you have retained evidence that you are the prior inventor and you can prove that your opponent derived the invention from you.

Supporting Tax Deductions

If an inventor can prove that he or she is in the "inventing business," then expenditures are deductible from ordinary income received. For IRS purposes, inventing (or any other activity) qualifies as a business if the primary motive for inventing is to earn a profit and if the inventor engages in inventing continuously and regularly over a substantial time period. If the inventor is audited, the IRS is more inclined to allow these deductions if the inventor can support them with clear and accurate documentation records of all invention activities, including conception, building, and testing, and expenditures for materials such as tools.

Lab Notebook

The most reliable and useful way to document an invention is to use a permanently bound notebook with the pages consecutively numbered, usually known as a lab notebook. Engineering and laboratory supply stores sell these notebooks with lines at the bottom of each page for signatures and signature dates of the inventor and the witnesses. A standard crackle-finish school notebook is also suitable, provided that the inventor numbers all of the pages consecutively, and has each page or each invention description dated, signed, and witnessed.

The inventor's lab notebook usually includes:

- descriptions of the invention and novel features
- procedures used in the building and testing of the invention
- drawings, photos, or sketches of the invention
- test results and conclusions
- discussions of any known prior-art references, and
- additional documentation, such as correspondence and purchase receipts.

27

TITLE: Self-Adjusting Can Opener - Building & Testing

REFERENCE: Conception recorded on page 23.

DESCRIPTION: A working model of this opener was made for me by Fred Smith
of Model Makers, Inc., starting Sept. 1. It was finished Sept. 13. It was made of
cold-rolled steel, 13 mm. thick, with brass bearings [etc.] . . .

Here is the photo we took on Sept. 15:

Locking groove ⎯ ⎯ Sliding clamp

PHOTO

RAMIFICATIONS: We also tried a nylon hinge, but it did not work because . . .

TEST DESCRIPTION: We tried the opener on fifty different cans, from size ___
to size ___ . . .

TEST RESULTS: For the size ___ cans, the opener worked as well as the Ajax
brand, opening each can in an average time of 8.3 seconds, the same as we
obtained with the Ajax brand. [etc.] . . .

INVENTOR: DATED:

Irma Inventor   20XX/8/27

THE ABOVE CONFIDENTIAL INFORMATION IS WITNESSED AND UNDERSTOOD:

Steve Elias   20XX/9/27

Fred Friendly   20XX/9/27

Figure 3A—Sample Notebook Page

RESOURCE

Lab notebooks can be purchased through Eureka Lab Book, Inc. (www.eurekalabbook.com) or Scientific Notebook Company (www.snco.com).

How to Enter Information in the Notebook

Entries must be handwritten and must accurately describe how events occurred. All entries must be dated as of the date the entry is made or must include an explanation for any delays in making an entry. The inventor must sign every entry. Computer printouts or other items that can't be entered directly in the notebook can be signed, dated, and witnessed, and then pasted or affixed in the notebook in chronological order. Photos or other entries that can't be signed are pasted in the notebook with a permanent adhesive and referenced by legends using descriptive words, such as "photo taken of machine in operation," made directly in the notebook. Draw in lead lines that extend from the notebook page over onto the photo to prevent a charge of substituting subsequently made photos. These pages are signed, dated, and witnessed in the usual manner. An item covering an entire page should be referred to on an adjacent page. A sketch drawn in pencil should be photocopied and affixed in the inventor's notebook in order to preserve a permanent copy.

Witnessing the Notebook

All notebook entries should be witnessed because an inventor's own testimony, even if supported by a properly completed notebook, will often be inadequate for proving an entry date.

The witnesses do more than verify the inventor's signature; they actually read or view and understand the technical subject material in the notebook, including the actual tests if they are witnessing the building and testing. For this reason, the chosen witnesses should have the ability or background to understand the invention. If the invention is a very simple mechanical device, practically anyone will have the technical qualifications to be a witness. But if it involves advanced chemical or electronic concepts, a witness must possess adequate background in the field. If called upon later, the witnesses must be able to testify to their own knowledge that the facts of the entry are correct.

While one witness may be sufficient, two are preferred because this enhances the likelihood of at least one of them being available to testify at a later date. If both are available, the inventor's case will be even stronger.

Some notebooks already contain a line for the inventor's signature and date on each page, together with the words "Witnessed and Understood" with lines for two signatures and dates. If the inventor's notebook doesn't already contain these words and signature lines, the inventor should write them in.

To preserve the trade secret status of the inventor's invention, the inventor should add the words "The above confidential information is" just before the words "Witnessed and Understood." An inventor who does not wish to rely on witnesses can still document reduction to practice by filing a provisional patent application (PPA) with the PTO.

Invention Disclosure

As an alternative to a lab notebook, an inventor can record conception, building, and testing on one or more sheets of paper in a form known as an "Invention Disclosure." (See Fig. 3B, below.) The inventor describes the invention including its title, purpose, advantages, novel features, and construction. If it has been built and tested, the results are recorded. The description of the invention is signed and dated by the inventor and preferably by two witnesses. If an inventor conceives of an invention on one date, and builds and tests the invention later, the inventor should make two separate invention disclosures.

Invention Disclosure

Sheet ___1___ of ___1___

Inventor(s): ___Irma Inventor___

Address(es): ___1919 Chestnut St., Philadelphia, PA 19103___

Title of Invention: ___Self-Adjusting Can Opener___

To record **Conception**, describe: 1. Circumstances of conception, 2. Purposes and advantages of invention, 3. Description, 4. Sketches, 5. Operation, 6. Ramifications, 7. Possible novel features, and 8. Closest known prior art. To record **Building and Testing**, describe: 1. Any previous disclosure of conception, 2. Construction, 3. Ramifications, 4. Operation and Tests, and 5. Test results. Include sketches and photos, where possible. Continue on additional identical copies of this sheet if necessary; inventors and witnesses should sign all sheets.

I thought of this can opener while at my friend Roberta's wedding last Sunday. I saw the caterer having trouble opening small and large cans with several openers. Thinking there was a better way, I recalled my Majestic KY3 sewing machine clamp and how it was adjustable and thought to modify the left arm to accommodate a can opener head.

My can opener will work with all sizes of cans and is actually cheaper than the most common existing one, the UR4 made by Ideal Co. of Racine, WI.

My can opener comprises a sliding clamp 10, a pincer groove 12, [etc.] as shown in the following sketch:

Sketch:

Operation: The user operates the can opener in the same way as any squeeze-and-turn opener for any size can.

Instead of sliding clamp 10, I can use a special notch as follows:

I believe that the combination of sliding clamp 10 and pincer groove 12 is a new one for can openers. Also I believe that it may be novel to provide a frammis head with my whatsit.

The Acme KZ122 can opener, mfgd. by Acme Kitchenwares of Berkeley, CA, and p. 417 of "Kitchen Tools & Their Uses" (Ready Publishers, Phila. 1981) show the closest can openers to my invention, in addition to the devices already mentioned.

Inventor(s): ___Irma Inventor___ Date: __20XX__ / __Jul__ / __6__

_____ Date: _____ / _____ / _____

The following understand, have witnessed, and agree not to disclose the above confidential information:

___Griselda Hammelfarb___ Date: __20xx__ / __Jul__ / __7__

___Neonore Zimla___ Date: __20xx__ / __Jul__ / __10__

Figure 3B—Invention Disclosure

> ### The "Post Office Patent"
>
> There's a myth that an inventor can document conception by mailing a description of the invention to him or herself by certified (or registered) mail and keeping the sealed envelope. The PTO has ruled that such "Post Office Patents" have little legal value.

Trade Secret Considerations

Developing and testing an invention should not compromise the trade secret status of the invention. For example, the notebook should be shown only to those persons willing to maintain its confidentiality. There is an implied understanding that witnesses must maintain confidentiality when signing the lab notebook.

Some inventors prefer that witnesses also sign a confidentiality agreement, sometimes known as a "nondisclosure," "keep confidential," or "proprietary materials" agreement. These agreements establish a legally binding confidential relationship between the parties. Inventors may also enter into confidentiality agreements with vendors of supplies, prototype makers, manufacturers, and companies that want to commercialize the invention. Although a confidentiality agreement will ensure the inventor's right to sue someone who discloses confidential information, it will not guarantee success in court. The inventor must also be able to prove that reasonable steps were taken to protect the confidential information and that the information has not become known to the public.

Patent Searching

Principles of Patent Searching

In this chapter we explain how attorneys, inventors, and businesses locate information about patents and related prior-art publications. Patent searches usually fall into three categories: bibliographic, patentability, and validity.

- **Bibliographic search.** This type of patent search retrieves items that you have already identified. For example, someone developing an invention may wish to review all of the patents in the field of the invention, or just a specific patent in the field. Alternatively, a company hiring an engineer may want to locate all of the patented inventions created by the prospective employee. A bibliographic search can often be done for free online.
- **Patentability search.** This type of search is performed to determine if an invention is likely to qualify for a patent. It requires examining current and expired patents and other related prior art to determine if the invention is nonobvious or novel. If the search indicates that an invention is likely to qualify, the inventor can develop, market, license, or sell the invention with some assurance that a patent will issue.
- **Validity search.** This type of search is made when one company sues another for patent infringement. It is usually more exhaustive than a patentability search because the company being sued is trying to prove that the PTO made a mistake when it issued the patent and the patent is therefore invalid.

Patentability and validity searches usually are made at the PTO in Alexandria, Virginia, where U.S. patents are searchable using the PTO's comprehensive EAST (Exam Assisted Searching Tool) system.

Although not as thorough, patent searching can be done using the Patent and Trademark Depository Libraries (PTDLs) located in major cities, or by using online patent databases. The best online search engine is Google Patents (https://patents.google.com). Also, the PTO provides online searching at its website (www.uspto.gov).

A search can be performed by a professional searcher, or you can do it yourself. Some inventors prefer to combine both techniques by doing the search themselves and also having a professional search done to double-check their work. Some inventors do a preliminary search, that is, locate patents by computer searching, and then hire a professional searcher for a more extensive search.

Patent Searches Are Never Perfect

Even when a professional search is made at the PTO, there are limitations. No search results are 100% certain for a variety of reasons:

- There is no way to search pending patent applications, with the exception of those published under the 18-month rule (see Chapter 1).
- The USPTO's search engine does not contain foreign, nonpatent, or exotic references.
- Very recently issued patents may not have been placed in the computer search files yet.
- Sometimes computer searching is done by class and subclass instead of by keywords, but patents may not be classified in the proper class or classified in an expected way.
- An invention may have been used publicly (without being published), or it may have been previously invented by an inventor who did not abandon, suppress, or conceal it.
- The searcher's choice of keywords may not correspond with the words used by the author of a relevant patent.

Hiring a Patent Searcher

There are two types of professional patent searchers: those who are licensed to practice before the PTO (patent attorneys and agents) and those who are not licensed. As a general rule, better results are obtained from patent attorneys and patent agents because they understand the concept of nonobviousness and novelty and often dig deeper than might at first appear necessary. Patent attorneys and agents are also licensed to express opinions on patentability.

Unlicensed searchers have one big advantage: They charge about half of what most attorneys and agents charge. Before hiring an unlicensed searcher, find out about the searcher's cost framework, technical background, on-the-job experience, usual amount of time spent on a search, and how the searcher searches (for example, whether the searcher contacts an examiner).

Most importantly, ask for the names of some clients so that you can check with them. Keep in mind that unlicensed searchers are not authorized to express opinions on patentability.

A "patent agent" has some technical training, generally an undergraduate degree in engineering, and is licensed by the PTO to prepare and prosecute patent applications. A patent agent can conduct a patent search and is authorized to express an opinion on patentability, but cannot appear in court and cannot handle licensing or infringement lawsuits. Patent attorneys must be licensed by the PTO and a licensing authority (such as the state bar or state supreme court) of at least one state. A "general" lawyer licensed to practice in one or more states, but not before the PTO, is not authorized to prepare patent applications or use the title "patent attorney."

Fees for patent searches range from $100 to $1,000 for searches by unlicensed searchers, and between $300 and $2,000 for searches by licensed patent attorneys or agents, not including an opinion on patentability. Some patent searchers charge a flat fee; others charge by the hour. If you plan to do much of the work yourself, you'll usually want hourly billing.

Locating a Searcher

Most patent searchers can be located through Internet search engines under "Patent Searchers." Searchers also advertise in periodicals such as the *Journal of the Patent and Trademark Office Society*, published by a private association of patent examiners. All patent agents and attorneys are listed at the PTO's website (https://oedci.uspto.gov). Most patent attorneys and agents who do searching in the PTO can be found in the District of Columbia section or the Virginia section under ZIP code 22202. Generally, hiring an attorney or agent in your locality to do the search is inefficient because the attorney or agent will have to hire an associate in or travel to Alexandria to conduct the search.

Preparing the Searcher

When furnishing a search request to a searcher, include the following:
- a clear and complete description of the invention
- drawings
- a copy of a related patent to identify the appropriate class to be searched
- identification of the novel features, and
- any required deadlines.

If using a patent attorney or agent, a search request will not compromise any trade secret status of the invention because by law it's considered a confidential communication. This simply means that the patent attorney or agent is required to keep your invention a secret. If you are using an unlicensed searcher, the law does not presume the disclosure is confidential, so you should ask your searcher to sign a confidentiality agreement, a contract in which one or both parties agree not to disclose certain information.

Reviewing the Search Results

After completing a search, a searcher usually furnishes:
- a list of the patents and other references discovered during the search
- a brief discussion of the cited patents and other references, pointing out the relevant parts of each, and
- a list of the classes and subclasses searched and the examiners consulted, if any.

The searcher will enclose copies of the references (usually U.S. patents, but possibly also foreign patents, magazine articles, and other published materials) cited in the search report. (For information about reading a patent, see Chapter 5.) If a patent attorney or agent has been hired to search, they will render an opinion as to patentability for an additional fee, usually $300 to $1,000.

The determination of whether an invention is patentable rarely comes in the form of a "yes" or "no" answer, unless the invention is a very simple device, process, or composition. Many inventions are complex enough to have some features, or some combination of features, that will be different enough to be patentable. However, the inventor's goal is not merely to get a patent, but to get meaningful patent coverage—that is, offensive rights that are broad enough that competitors can't "design around" the patent easily. Designing around a patent is the act of making a competitive device or process that is equivalent in function to the patented device but that doesn't infringe the patent.

After the search results are evaluated, the inventor has a pretty good idea of the minimum number of novel features that are necessary to sufficiently distinguish the invention over the prior art. The scope of patent coverage—that is, how narrow or broad the claims—is determined by the novel features that distinguish an invention over the prior art and provide new results that are different or unexpected enough to be considered nonobvious. The fewer the novel features needed to distinguish the invention, the broader the scope of coverage. Stated differently, if many new features are needed to distinguish the invention from prior art, the coverage is narrow and it's usually easier for a competitor to provide the same results without infringing.

Do-It-Yourself Searching

The best place to make a search of the patent files is in the PTO, unless you have access to the files of a large company that specializes in your field. This is because the PTO's search facilities have the EAST (Exam Assisted Searching Tool) system on its computers. Unfortunately, the PTO no longer classifies foreign patents and literature along with U.S. patents according to subject matter. The PTO libraries are open to the public and any inventor can travel to Virginia and perform a search using the PTO EAST system. Although not as thorough, searches can also be performed using the facilities of PTDLs (Patent and Trademark Depository Libraries) located in major U.S. cities, or by using online patent databases.

Search Prerequisites: Terminology and Classification

Regardless of whether you are performing a simple search or an extensive search, there are two prerequisites: You must articulate the terms that describe the nature and essence of the invention, and then find the relevant classifications or Boolean search terms for the invention.

In order to properly search for patents, you must be familiar with the elements of a patent, such as the specification, claims, and abstract. (For information on patent elements, read Chapter 5.)

Terms That Describe the Invention

In the PTO files, patents, like any indexed system, are classified using keywords (terms) and classifications. Successful patent searching is dependent on using the same words and phrases that coincide with the terms used by the PTO classifier or indexer, or the patent's author. For example, if artificial rainmaking machines are indexed by "rainfall simulation," you will have a difficult time locating patents under "artificial rain." For this reason, you must first figure out several ways to describe the invention, then extract the terminology from those descriptions in order to locate similar inventions. For example, if you're searching for patents relating to a bicycle with a new type of sprocket wheel, write down "bicycle, sprocket wheel," and any additional terms. In the computer search systems at the PTO and elsewhere, these terms are called Boolean terms because the computer searches for relevant patents using Boolean logic. Boolean logic is a searching method in which terms are joined by using connectors such as AND, OR, and NOT (for example, "Bicycle AND Wheel").

Classification for the Invention

In addition to appropriate terminology, you also need to determine the invention's most relevant search classification, called class and subclass. Every type of invention is categorized in a class. For example, if you invented something that has to do with sewing, you would search the patents in Class 112. If the invention had to do with sewing gloves, it would be in Class 112, Subclass 16. You can find the appropriate classifications in any of the following references, all of which are available on the PTO website. These consist of:

- *Index to the U.S. Patent Classification.* Lists all possible subject areas of invention alphabetically, from "abacus" to "zwieback," together with the appropriate class and subclass for each. The *Index* also lists the classes alphabetically.
- *Manual of Classification.* Lists all classes numerically and subclasses under each class. After locating the class and subclass numbers, the *Manual of Classification* is used as an adjunct to the *Index* to check the selected classes and to find other, closely related ones.
- *Classification Definitions.* Contains a definition for every class and subclass in the *Manual of Classification.* At the end of each subclass definition is a cross-reference to additional places to look that correspond to the subclass. A local PTDL will have the Classification And Search Support Information System (CASSIS) on CD-ROM, where search classifications can be found.

Searching at the PTO

The PTO is physically located in the Carlyle Complex at Eisenhower and Duke Streets in Alexandria, Virginia. The PTO is technically part of the Department of Commerce (headquartered in Washington) but operates in an almost autonomous fashion.

The primary advantage of searching at the PTO is that you have access to the PTO's EAST searching system. Access to the EAST system and assignment search systems is available to the public without charge. Staff members can assist customers in locating appropriate files and reference materials. In addition to patent copies, the PTO search facilities maintain a variety of paper reference materials, including manuals, indexes, dictionaries, reference publications, and the *Official Gazette.* The *Official Gazette* is published online each Tuesday to announce those patents being issued, and those trademarks being registered or published for opposition. Volumes relating specifically to patents or trademarks are available in the corresponding search facility.

Search EAST and WEST

In addition to searching at the PTO's specialized EAST computer terminals, you can also make computer searches on specialized WEST (Web-based Examiner Search Tool) terminals in certain Patent and Trademark Depository Libraries, or on a personal computer connected to the Internet.

EAST is the superior search tool because it can perform a search by class and subclass, similar to the search of paper patents described above. Users of EAST can also make Boolean or keyword combination searches back to 1836, or make searches using a combination of both techniques. In terms of speed, it is superior to a paper search because you can flip through patents displayed on the computer monitor faster than the actual paper copies. You can also use EAST to do "forward" searches—that is, if a relevant patent is found, EAST can find and search through all later-issued patents in which the relevant patent is cited (referred to) as a prior-art reference. Further, it can do "backward" searches—that is, it can search through all previously issued patents that are cited as prior art in the relevant patent. You can also use EAST to search European and Japanese patents.

EAST is free to use at the PTO, but the PTO charges for printing out copies of patents. The PTDLs that have WEST charge hourly fees.

At the beginning of 2019, the PTO employed almost 12,500 total people, including 8,185 patent examiners and 579 trademark examiners. All patent examiners have technical undergraduate degrees, in such fields as electrical engineering, chemistry, and physics. Many examiners are also attorneys. Examiners review patent applications and determine whether inventions meet the standard of patentability.

Assuming you do go to the PTO in Alexandria, you can make the search using the EAST system in the public search room, referred to as the Public Patent Search and Image Retrieval Facility (PSIRF). Also, you may visit the examiners in the actual examining division to consult with an examiner responsible for the technical area of your invention.

If you need help with the search, you can ask any of the search assistants in the search room or an examiner in the actual examining division. The security of the invention won't be endangered by providing the details to PTO employees because they are not allowed to file patent applications.

Searching in a Patent and Trademark Depository Library

If you can't make it to Virginia, the next best option is to search in one of the Patent and Trademark Depository Libraries listed on the PTO website (www.uspto.gov). Before going to any PTDL, call to find out their hours of operation and what search facilities they offer.

Aside from the problem of travelling to the PTO, searches at a PTDL are usually more difficult than at the PTO because PTDLs do not have the same support staff that the PTO has and because the EAST system is somewhat inferior to the WEST system. Both systems lack foreign patents and nonpatent literature—for example, books, magazines, and other published materials. (Note: The PTO no longer puts foreign patent and nonpatent literature in the search files.) In general, using a PTDL is more difficult and time-consuming than using the PTO facilities in Virginia.

The PTO periodically publishes CD-ROM discs that contain information about patents. Most PTDLs subscribe to these discs and have one or more computers with CD-ROM drives for reading the discs. Because the discs contain only classification and bibliographic information, they can't be used to make a true patentability search. They can be used as a searching aid and to provide other information about patents that you may find useful. The two most helpful discs are:

- **CASSIS/CLASS discs** (patents from 1790 to the present). These can be used to find the classification of any patent or the list of patents in any class. However, this information can also now be accessed at the PTO's website.

- **CASSIS/BIB discs** (patents from 1980 to the present). These can be used to find the classification of any recently issued patent, to find all patents assigned to any company or individual, to find a list of patents by year of issue, status (expired, reexamined, etc.), all patents by inventor's residence, all recently issued patents with a certain word or words in their title or abstract (this feature can be used to perform a crude search), and to find the field of search (class and subclass) for any type of invention. Again, this information can also be accessed online at the PTO's website.

Searching the *Official Gazette*

The *Official Gazette* or patents (the *OG*) is an online periodical published weekly by the PTO at its website www.uspto.gov. The publication lists the main facts (patentee, assignee, filing date, classification) plus the broadest claim and main drawing figure of every patent issued that week. It also contains pertinent notices, fees, and a list of all PTDLs. It is possible to perform a preliminary search using the *OG* located at a PTDL (or at the PTO) and it is generally easier than using CASSIS because each patent entry in the *OG* contains only a single claim (or abstract) and a single figure or drawing of the patent.

For each patent, the *OG* entry gives the patent number, inventor's name and address, assignee (usually a company that the inventor has transferred ownership of the patent to), filing date, application serial number, international classification, U.S. classification, number of claims, and a sample claim or abstract. If the drawing and claim look relevant, go to the actual patent online or order a copy of it. The claim found in the *Official Gazette* is the essence of the claimed invention, not a descriptive summary of the technical information in the patent. Therefore, even if a patent's *Official Gazette* claim doesn't precisely describe the invention, the rest of the patent may still contain technical information that is relevant.

Obtaining Copies of Patents

You can download a copy of any U.S. patent from:

- the U.S. Patent and Trademark Office (http://patft.uspto.gov)
- Google Patents (https://patents.google.com)
- Free Patents Online (www.freepatentsonline.com), or
- Pat2PDF (www.pat2pdf.org).

These sites will deliver a PDF copy of the entire patent right to your computer desktop. You can also order foreign and U.S. patent copies from a private supply company, such as Derwent Innovation (https://clarivate.com/products/derwent-innovation).

Computer Searching

Here's how to obtain access to various patent databases:

- **The PTO's EAST (Exam Assisted Searching Tool) system.** This is available at the PTO in Alexandria, Virginia, and is the best search tool. Free to use, but requires some training. This system searches all U.S. patents back to 1836 and is the paramount computer patent search system. There is no charge for using the EAST system and instructions and help are available at the PTO's search room.
- **The WEST system (available at PTDLs).** Very good but not as good as the EAST terminals. Most Patent and Trademark Depository Libraries (PTDLs) charge to use their WEST terminals.
- **Google Patents (https://patents.google.com)** is an excellent resource that includes U.S. patents back to the beginning. We strongly recommend this site.
- **The PTO's Search System (http://patft.uspto.gov).** A free search system that can search patents and published patent applications separately but goes back to 1976 only.

Figure 4A—Screenshot From *Official Gazette*

- **The European Patent Office's Search System (www.epo.org/searching-for-patents.html).** A free search system that can search U.S., European, and Japanese patents and published applications as far back as the 1920s.

If you are going to do the search yourself, we strongly recommend that you include the last search system above—the EPO—because it covers many patents that the U.S.-based search systems do not include.

Several fee-based organizations offer computer searching of patent records and some provide foreign patent information:

- **Clarivate Analytics (https://clarivate.com).** Formerly the Derwent commercial database of U.S. and international patents, this service also includes patent analysis research tools.

- **Total Patent (www.lexisnexis.com/totalpatent).** Formerly known as LexPat, this commercial patent database offers extensive prior-art searching capability of technical journals and magazines, and includes patent optimization tools.
- **Questel/Orbit (www.questel.com)** provides a collection of intellectual property databases as well as consulting and legal services.
- **Ip.com (www.ip.com)** is a service that uses "concept" or "semantic" searching that is more complete than traditional Boolean searching and encompasses many databases.

Computer Searching Terminology

Most computer search systems do not group and search patents by PTO classification. Instead, they search solely for combinations of key words in the text of the patent, a method of searching known as Boolean searching.

For example, consider a bicycle invention with a frame made of a certain carbon fiber alloy. If searching at the PTO, the searcher would look through the patents in the bike and metallurgical (carbon fiber alloy) classifications. However, if searching for the same invention online, the searcher would select a combination of keywords (such as "bicycle" and "carbon fiber alloy") and the search engine would identify any patents that contain the keywords.

The search may result in finding too many irrelevant patents, in which case the search can be narrowed by using more specific keywords. However, if the search words are too specific, the search engine is likely to report no patents, or just one or two. The PTO's examiners presently use computer searching to supplement their searches.

Before searching a database, thoroughly study the service's instruction manual or online help program. If using a fee-based database, this will help to keep costs down. Although every system is different, the following terms are common to all systems:

- **File.** The name of the patent search database provided by the service.
- **Record.** A portion of a file. The term is used to designate a single reference, usually a patent, within the database.

- **Field.** A portion of a record, such as a patent's title, the names of the inventors, its filing date, its patent number, its claims, and more.
- **Term.** A group or, in computer-speak, a "string" of characters within a field (for example, the inventor's surname or one word of the patent title are all terms).
- **Command.** An instruction or directive to the search system that tells it to perform a function (for example, "Search" might be a command to tell a system to look for some keywords in its database).
- **Keyword or Search Term.** Words that are actually searched (for example, "bicycle" and "carbon fiber alloy" are keywords we've used in examples above).
- **Qualifier.** A symbol that is used to limit a search or the information that the search displays. Normally no qualifier would be used in novelty searches, but if you're looking for a patent from a certain inventor, you could add a qualifier that limits your search to the field of the inventor's name.
- **Wild Card Symbol.** A symbol that is used in place of a word's normal ending in order to broaden a keyword (for example, if the wild card were an asterisk (*) and you typed "Auto*" your search would display "automobile," "automotive," "automatic," and any other word that started with the prefix "auto").
- **Connector Word.** A word such as "OR," "AND," and "NOT" that tells the computer to look for certain defined logical or Boolean combinations of keywords. For instance, if you type in a command telling the computer to search for "annulus OR ring AND napkin," the computer would recognize that "OR" and "AND" were connector words, and would search for patents with the words "annulus" and "napkin," or "ring" and "napkin," in combination.
- **Proximity Symbol.** Tells the computer to look for specified keywords, provided they are not more than a certain number of terms apart. Thus, if you told the computer to search for "napkin w/5 shaping" it would look for any patent that contained

the words "napkin" and "shaping" within five words of each other, the symbol "w/5" meaning "within five words of." If no proximity symbol is used and the words are placed adjacent to each other—such as "napkin shaping"—the computer will retrieve only those patents that contain these two words adjacent to each other in the order given. However, if a connector word is used—such as "napkin AND shaping"—the computer will pull out any patent with both of these words, no matter where they are in the patent and no matter in what order they appear.

Alternative Search Terms

No matter what online search system you use, be prepared with a group of keywords and possible synonyms or equivalents. Use a thesaurus or a visual dictionary to get synonyms. Thus, to search for a napkin-shaping ring, in addition to the obvious key words "ring," "napkin," and "shaping," think of other terms from the same and analogous fields. In addition to napkin, you could use "cloth." Or, in addition to shaping, you could use "folding" or "bending."

Patent Searching Techniques

To give you an idea of how online searching works, let's proceed through a search using the PTO's patent database. To begin any search at the PTO website, access the home page at www.uspto.gov, and then click "Patents" or "Search for Patents." You are directed to an option entitled "Patent Full-Text and Full-Page Image Databases." You can elect to search either "Patent Grants" for current patents or "Patent Applications" if you wish to search published patent applications. Let's assume you were searching for prior-art patents related to hot-air popcorn poppers. There are four ways to search both databases: Boolean search, manual search, patent number search, and class and subclass search:

- **Boolean search.** This type of search is accomplished by using terms, fields, and connectors. As you can see from Fig. 4C, the Boolean searching system has been simplified to some extent so you can select the connector term ("AND," "OR," "AND

NOT") from a drop-down menu. You can initiate a search for hot-air popcorn poppers by searching for patents with the words "popcorn AND air" anywhere in the patent. The Google Patent search engine is a Boolean system and works similarly to the PTO and other search systems.

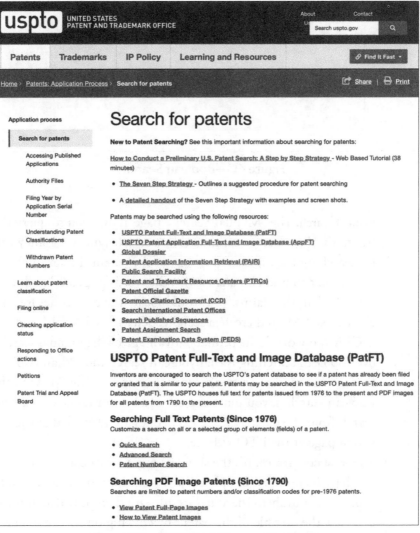

Figure 4B—PTO Web Patent Database

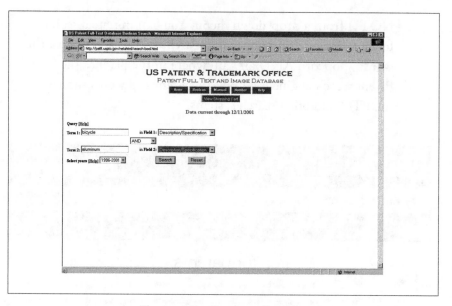

Figure 4C—Boolean Search

- **Manual search.** The "Manual Search" page allows you to query the patent database using "command line search syntax," a fancy title for searching the different portions of the patent. For example, if you want to find all patents with the word "popcorn" and the word "air" in the claims, you would locate the field codes for the claims (ACLM) and create a search, such as "ACLM/air" and "ACLM/popcorn." The primary advantage of the manual search over Boolean searching is that you can search more than two fields or use more than two search terms at one time. As with the Boolean searches, you must also select a year or range of years to search from the database. The field codes are identified in each search page at the PTO website.

- **Patent number search.** It's the simplest way to locate a patent if you have its number. Simply click "Patent Number Search" and type in the number. The search results are then provided and you can view the text file of the patent by clicking on its name. For example, if you wanted to view the design patent for a hot-air popcorn popper and had only the number, you would type in the number in the search field and the text of the patent would be displayed. You can view the actual images by clicking "Images."

- **Class-and-subclass search.** This type of search differs from the first three types in that keywords are not used. Instead you must locate the appropriate class and subclass where patents that might disclose your invention (or developments close to it) are located and look at all of the patents in the subclass. This method of searching is obviously not as efficient as the former three keyword searches but nevertheless some searchers find it useful as a double-check or when they aren't sure of the appropriate keywords to put into the search engine. We will not provide detailed instructions on class-and-subclass searching here since it isn't too popular anymore, but you can find out more in *Patent It Yourself* and from the search assistants in the PTO's search room. To make a class-and-subclass search, you must first find the classes and subclasses where your invention is classified. To do this, you may avail yourself of the PTO's *Manual of Classification*, the *Classification Definitions Manual*, and the *Index To Classification*. Once armed with the likely classes and subclasses, go to the PTO's search site (http://patft.uspto. gov) and use the "Advanced Search" link to retrieve all patents in each selected class and subclass. For example, if you want to search in Class 705, Subclass 39, enter CCL/705/39 in the "Query" box and the engine will return a list of all patents that are so classified. (Don't forget to make a search of both Patents and "Patent Applications.") You'll then have to view each patent individually to see if any of them disclose your brainchild or any feature of it.

Reading and Writing Patents

Patents are written in a formal, stylized manner packed with legal and scientific terminology. The claims within the patent are written in an arcane style that is positively puzzling to the uninitiated. That's the bad news. The good news is that, with patience, any patent can be interpreted. The purpose of this chapter is to introduce you to the various elements of a patent and discuss how a patent application is prepared.

Elements of an Issued Patent

The key elements of an issued patent are: (1) data about the inventor, application serial number, filing and issue dates, and related information; (2) the specification (this consists of (a) the background leading up to the invention, (b) a description of the invention, (c) the claims, and (d) the abstract); and (3) the drawings. The drawings and the description explain the background of and how to make and use the invention, and the claims define the scope or boundaries of the patent. Specifications for patents issued since 1971 must include an abstract that summarizes the invention. All patent applications must include a drawing if the subject matter permits. However, some applications, such as those for pure chemicals, don't include a drawing unless the invention is a process that can be diagrammed by a flowchart. We will discuss these five elements in the following sections. We will also discuss the additional materials required when submitting a patent application.

Invention and Inventor Data

The first page of the patent provides the inventor's name, the name of any assignee (a person or company to whom the inventor may have transferred ownership), the application filing date, the application serial number, the patent issue date, the patent number, any related prior applications (domestic and foreign), the fields of invention that were searched, and any relevant prior art cited in the search (see Chapter 4).

Specification

The "description" part of the specification discloses how to make and use an invention, and the "claims" part of the specification states the metes and bounds of the invention claimed so that anyone can determine whether any device or process infringes the patent. Every specification must describe the invention so that someone with ordinary skill in the field of the invention can make and use it without any significant further experimenting. The specification must also disclose the "best mode," or the best way, of creating and using the invention. If the inventor knew of a better way and failed to disclose it, that failure previously could result in the loss of patent rights, but under the America Invents Act (AIA), failure to disclose the best mode is no longer a fatal flaw.

> **EXAMPLE:** In 1978, an inventor at United States Gypsum (USG) conceived of a formula for a joint compound used to fill the joints between adjacent gypsum wallboards. One of the ingredients in the formula was a silicon-treated substance called Sil-42. When discussing the compound with USG's patent attorney, the inventor listed Sil-42 as a component, but before the patent application was filed, a USG executive instructed the attorney to omit any reference to Sil-42. After the patent was issued, USG sued National Gypsum for infringement of its joint compound patent. The court held that the patent was invalid because, by omitting the silicon substance, USG failed to disclose the best mode of making the joint compound. (*United States Gypsum Co. v. National Gypsum Co.*, 74 F.3d 1209 (CAFC 1996).)
>
> Today, under the AIA, the omission of the reference to Sil-42 would usually not be fatal. (But keep in mind that if the Sil-42 was an important component of the compound, such that the benefits of the invention would be lost without it, its omission would today still be regarded as a fatal failure to disclose how to make and use the invention.)

Elements of the Specification

According to PTO Rule 77 (37 Code of Federal Regulations § 1.77), the specification should consist of the following elements:

- title
- cross-reference to related application(s) (if any)
- federally sponsored research and development (if any)
- background of the invention (usually includes a discussion of prior art and the advantages of the invention)
- summary (usually a one-paragraph description of the invention as claimed)
- brief description of drawings
- detailed description of the invention and how to make and use it computer program (if any)
- claims and abstract (although legally part of the specification, popular usage and this book treat them as separate parts of the application), and
- sequence listing for biotech inventions (if any).

The specification is supposed to have separate headings in capital letters (but not in boldface). The specification elements shown here reflect changes made in patent rules in 2000. Applications filed before this change include the same information although the headings in the published patent may differ.

Throughout this section, we will isolate each element of the specification and provide an example from a patent titled "Paper-Laminated Pliable Closure for Flexible Bags" (Pat. No. 4,783,886).

Title

The title is a short, simple summary of the invention—for example, "Paper-Laminated Pliable Closure for Flexible Bags" (Pat. No. 4,783,886). (See Fig. 5A, below.)

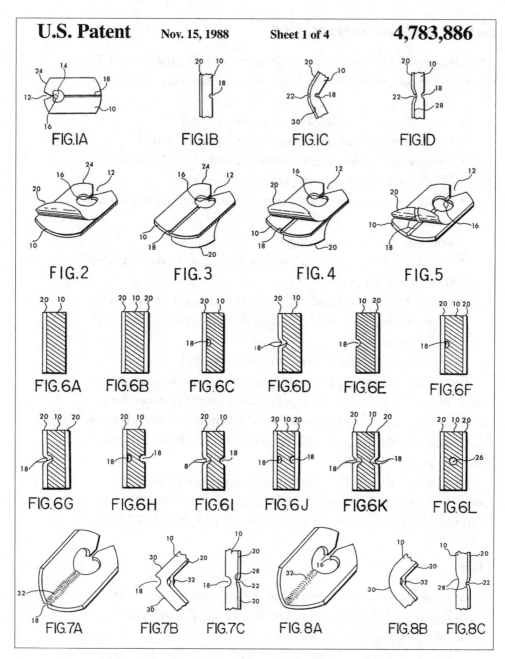

U.S. Patent   Nov. 15, 1988   Sheet 1 of 4   4,783,886

Figure 5A—Drawings of Sample Patent Application

> **TIP**
>
> **Patent numbers and codes.** Every U.S. patent since 1836 has been issued a patent number—for example, Pat. No. 5,152,062. Patent numbering started in 1836 and patent 10,800,000 issued December 15, 2020. When several patents are the subjects of litigation or interference, judges and attorneys refer to each patent by the last three digits of the registration—for example, the '062 patent. In recent years, patent numbers have also been published with codes that identify the kind of patent. These include: A1 (patent application was published before grant), B1 (issued patent was published before grant), B2 (patent was not published before grant), E (reissue patent), H (statutory invention registration), P2 (plant patent), and S (design patent).

Cross-References to Related Applications

If the inventor or an inventor in the same organization has any other patent applications on file relating to the current invention, these are listed in the "Cross-References" section. Cross-references are necessary if the applicant is seeking the benefit of the filing date of a prior application or wants to incorporate a disclaimer of another case. (See Chapter 6 for more information about when a cross-reference may be useful.) If there are no cross-references, this section can be omitted or the applicant may state, "Not applicable."

Federally Sponsored Research and Development

If the invention was made with government funding, the government will have rights in the invention and this will be indicated here. A typical statement may read, "This invention was made under a contract with the U.S. Department of Energy."

Sequence Listing or Program

If the invention uses a biotechnological sequence or a computer program, it will be indicated here and included, either in the specification or on a CD.

Background (Field of the Invention)

This section is no longer required and, under recent court decisions, it has been held limiting, so it should no longer be used.

Background (Discussion of Prior Art)

To demonstrate novelty and nonobviousness, it is desirable to distinguish the invention from the prior art. To do this, many practitioners list the prior art uncovered in a search and then criticize it by discussing its disadvantages. However, it is important never to disclose any prior development unless it exists, not to denigrate any prior development unless the criticism is truly justified, and not to mention any disadvantage of a prior-art reference unless your invention eliminates this disadvantage. For example:

Grocery stores and supermarkets commonly supply consumers with polyethylene bags for holding produce. Such bags are also used by suppliers to provide a resealable container for other items, both edible and inedible.

Originally these bags were sealed by the supplier with staples or by heat. However, consumers objected because these were of a rather permanent nature: The bags could be opened only by tearing, thereby damaging them and rendering them impossible to reseal.

Thereafter, inventors created several types of closures to seal plastic bags in such a way as to leave them undamaged after they were opened. U.S. patent 4,292,714 to Walker (1981) discloses a complex clamp, which can close the necks of bags without causing damage upon opening; however, these clamps are prohibitively expensive to manufacture.

U.S. patent 2,981,990 to Balderree (1961) shows a closure that is of expensive construction, being made of PTFE, and which is not effective unless the bag has a relatively long "neck." Thus if the bag has been filled almost completely and consequently has a short neck, this closure is useless. Also, being relatively narrow and clumsy, Balderree's closure cannot be easily bent by hand along its longitudinal axis. Finally, his closure does not hold well onto the bag, but has a tendency to snap off.

Although twist closures with a wire core are easy to use and inexpensive to manufacture, do not damage the bag upon being removed, and can be used repeatedly, they simply do not possess the neat and uniform appearance of a tab closure. They become tattered and unsightly after repeated use and do not offer suitable surfaces for the reception of print or labeling. These ties also require much more manipulation to apply and remove.

Several types of thin, flat closures have been proposed—for example, in U.K. patent 883,771 to Britt et al. (1961) and U.S. patents 3,164,250 (1965), 3,417,912 (1968), 3,822,441 (1974), 4,361,935 (1982), and 4,509,231 (1985), all to Paxton. Although inexpensive to manufacture, capable of use with bags having a short neck, and producible in break-off strips, such closures can be used only once if they are made of frangible plastic because they must be bent or twisted when being removed and consequently will fracture upon removal. Thus, to reseal a bag originally sealed with a frangible closure, one must either close its neck with another closure or else close it in makeshift fashion by folding or tying it. My own patent 4,694,542 (1987) describes a closure that is made of flexible plastic and is therefore capable of repeated use without damage to the bag, but nevertheless all the plastic closures heretofore known suffer from a number of disadvantages:

(a) Their manufacture in color requires the use of a compounding facility for the production of the pigmented plastic. Such a facility, which is needed to compound the primary pigments and which generally constitutes a separate production site, requires the presence of very large storage bins for the pigmented raw granules. Also, it presents great difficulties with regard to the elimination of the airborne powder that results from the mixing of the primary granules.

(b) If one uses an extruder in the production of a pigmented plastic— especially if one uses only a single extruder—a change from one color to a second requires purging the extruder of the granules having the first color by introducing those of the second color. This process inevitably produces, in sizeable volume, an intermediate product of an undesired color that must be discarded as scrap, thereby resulting in waste of material and time.

(c)   *The colors of the closures in present use are rather unsaturated. If greater concentrations of pigment were used in order to make the colors more intense, the plastic would become more brittle and the cost of the final product would increase.*

(d)   *The use of pigmented plastic closures does not lend itself to the production of multicolored designs, and it would be very expensive to produce plastic closures in which the plastic is multicolored— for example, in which the plastic has stripes of several colors, or in which the plastic exhibits multicolored designs.*

(e)   *Closures made solely of plastic generally offer poor surfaces for labeling or printing, and the label or print is often easily smudged.*

(f)   *The printing on a plastic surface is often easily erased, thereby allowing the alteration of prices by dishonest consumers.*

(g)   *The plastic closures in present use are slippery when handled with wet or greasy fingers.*

(h)   *A closure of the type in present use can be very carefully pried off a bag by a dishonest consumer and then attached to another item without giving any evidence of such removal.*

Advantages

The invention's advantages are listed to sell the invention and show how it is superior over the prior art. In some ways, this section is the converse of the disadvantages described in the prior art discussion.

There is a growing trend among patent attorneys to either title this section simply as "Advantages," or eliminate the section entirely. Those attorneys who title it as "Advantages" often also include a disclaimer such as "Accordingly, the present invention may have one or more of the following advantages. . . ."

The reason for this trend is that some appellate courts have, during the past decade, limited the scope of patent rights based on statements made by the applicant in the "Objects" section of the "Objects and Advantages" portion of the specification. When the courts limit the patent claims it is often harder for the patent owner to prove infringement. Hence, many attorneys either avoid listing the objects or strike the entire section. (*Gentry Gallery, Inc. v. Berkline Corp.*, 134 F.3d 1473, 1479 (Fed. Cir. 1998) and *Vehicular Technologies Corp. v. Tital Wheel International, Inc.*, 212 F.3d 1377, 1380 (Fed. Cir. 2000).)

Regardless of whether "Advantages" continues to be a viable portion of the specification, we include it here because historically, it has been a common element of patent drafting and you are likely to see it in published patents. Also, there is a trend to eliminate use of the word "invention," because some courts have used this to limit the claims.

Accordingly, besides the advantages of the flexible closures described in my above patent, several advantages of one or more aspects of the present closure are as follows hereto:

(a) it can be produced in a variety of colors without requiring the manufacturer to use a compounding facility for the production of pigments

(b) it enables a convenient and extremely rapid and economical change of color in the closures that are being produced

(c) it is flexible and can be brightly colored

(d) it can be colored in several colors simultaneously

(e) it provides a superior surface for the reception of labeling or print

(f) its labeling cannot be altered

(g) it will not be slippery when handled with wet or greasy fingers, and

(h) it will show evidence of having been switched from one item to another by a dishonest consumer—in other words, to provide a closure that makes items tamper-proof.

Further advantages of one or more aspects are that it can be used easily and conveniently to open and reseal a plastic bag, without damage to the bag, which is simple to use and inexpensive to manufacture, which can be supplied in separate tabs en masse or in break-off links, which can be used with bags having short necks, which can be used repeatedly, and which obviates the need to tie a knot in the neck of the bag or fold the neck under the bag or use a twist closure. Still further advantages of various aspects will become apparent from a consideration of the ensuing description and drawings.

Summary

The specification must contain a summary of the invention:

A bag closure comprises a flat body having a notch, a gripping aperture adjacent to the notch, and a layer of paper laminated on its side.

Later on we'll discuss the abstract, which comes at the end of the specification. If you're thinking ahead, you may well ask, "Isn't it duplicative to provide what are in effect two synopses—the Summary and an Abstract?" We agree, but since the rules require both, we have no choice. Also, there is a difference: The Summary is supposed to be a summary of what is claimed (many attorneys simply paraphrase the main claim to write the summary) and the Abstract is supposed to be a summary of the entire disclosure.

Description of the Drawings

The description of the drawings provides a brief explanation of the different views or "figures" of the patent drawings (see Fig. 5A, above):

In the drawings, closely related figures have the same number but different alphabetic suffixes.

Figs. 1A to 1D show various aspects of a closure supplied with a longitudinal groove and laminated on one side with paper.

Fig. 2 shows a closure with no longitudinal groove and with a paper lamination on one side only.

Fig. 3 shows a similar closure with one longitudinal groove.

Fig. 4 shows a similar closure with a paper lamination on both sides.

Fig. 5 shows a similar closure with a paper lamination on one side only, the groove having been formed into the paper as well as into the body of the closure.

Figs. 6A to 6L show end views of closures having various combinations of paper laminations, longitudinal grooves, and through-holes.

Figs. 7A to 7C show a laminated closure with groove after being bent and after being straightened again.

Figs. 8A to 8C show a laminated closure without a groove after being bent and after being straightened again.

Detailed Description

This section describes the invention's structure and explains its performance. Usually, the description and operation are provided in two separate subparts, as reproduced below, but some inventions are not capable of physical descriptions and the two sections (description and operation) are merged, for example, as in a chemical process.

Description—preferred embodiment. The description is a discussion of the physical structure or static arrangement of the first or basic embodiment. It usually starts with the base, frame, bottom, input, or some other logical starting point, and then works up, out, or forward in a logical manner. Each part is named and numbered and is usually related to the numbering in the patent drawings. Previously, we explained that the specification must provide the best mode or embodiment of the invention. It is in this portion of the specification that the best mode is provided.

One embodiment of the closure is illustrated in Fig. 1A (top view) and Fig. 1B (end view). The closure has a thin base 10 of uniform cross section consisting of a flexible sheet of material that can be repeatedly bent and straightened out without fracturing. A layer of paper 20 (Fig. 1B) is laminated on one side of base 10. In the preferred embodiment, the base is a flexible plastic, such as poly-ethylene-tere-phthalate (PET—hyphens here supplied to facilitate pronunciation)—available from Eastman Chemical Co. of Kingsport, TN. However, the base can consist of any other material that can be repeatedly bent without fracturing, such as polyethylene, polypropylene, vinyl, nylon, rubber, leather, various impregnated or laminated fibrous materials, various plasticized materials, cardboard, paper, etc.

At one end of the closure is a lead-in notch 12, which terminates in gripping points 16 and leads to a hole 14. Paper layer 20 adheres to base 10 by virtue either of the extrusion of liquid plastic (which will form the body of the closure) directly onto the paper or the application of heat or adhesive upon the entirety of one side of base 10. The paper-laminated closure is then punched out. Thus the lamination will have the same shape as the side of the base 10 to which it adheres.

The base of the closure is typically .8 mm to 1.2 mm in thickness, and has overall dimensions roughly from 20 mm x 20 mm (square shape) to 40 mm x 70 mm (oblong shape). The outer four corners 24 of the closure are typically beveled or rounded to avoid snagging and personal injury. Also, when closure tabs are connected side-to-side in a long roll, these bevels or roundings give the roll a series of notches that act as detents or indices for the positioning and conveying of the tabs in a dispensing machine.

A longitudinal groove 18 is formed on one side of base 10 in Fig. 1. In other embodiments, there may be two longitudinal grooves—one on each side of the base—or there may be no longitudinal groove at all. Groove 18 may be formed by machining, scoring, rolling, or extruding. In the absence of a groove, there may be a longitudinal through-hole 26 (Fig. 6L). This through-hole may be formed by placing, in the extrusion path of the closure, a hollow pin for the outlet of air.

Description of additional or alternative embodiments. If there are several embodiments or several ways of operation, the specification should describe the most preferred or most basic embodiment and its operation first, then describe each additional or alternative embodiment in the same manner, but more briefly. However, we recommend that the word "first" and not "preferred" be used to refer to the first embodiment since some courts have tended to give less respect to nonpreferred embodiments.

Additional embodiment

Additional embodiments are shown in Figs. 2, 3, 4, and 5; in each case the paper lamination is shown partially peeled back. In Fig. 2 the closure has only one lamination and no groove; in Fig. 3 it has only one lamination and only one groove; in Fig. 4 it has two laminations and only one groove; in Fig. 5 it has two laminations and one groove, the latter having been rolled into one lamination as well as into the body of the closure.

Alternative embodiment

There are various possibilities with regard to the relative disposition of the sides that are grooved and the sides that are laminated, as illustrated in Fig. 6, which presents end views along the longitudinal axis. Fig. 6A shows a closure with lamination on one side only and with no groove; Fig. 6B shows a closure with laminations on both sides and with no groove; Fig. 6C shows a closure with laminations on only one groove, both being on the same side; Fig. 6D shows a closure with only one lamination and only one groove, both being on the same side and the groove having been rolled into the lamination as well as into the body of the closure; Fig. 6E shows a closure with only one lamination and only one groove, the two being on opposite sides; Fig. 6F shows a closure with two laminations and only one groove; Fig. 6G shows a closure with two laminations and only one groove, the groove having been rolled into one lamination as well as into the body of the closure; Fig. 6H shows a closure with only one lamination and with two grooves; Fig. 6I shows a closure with only one lamination and with two grooves, one of the grooves having been rolled into the lamination as well as into the body of the closure; Fig. 6J shows a closure with two laminations and with two grooves; Fig. 6K shows a closure with two laminations and with two grooves, the grooves having been rolled into the laminations as well as into the body of the closure; and Fig. 6L shows a closure with two laminations and a longitudinal through-hole.

Operation. Following the static description, the specification includes an "operation" section that describes the action of the basic embodiment's parts and how to use it. The operation section should not introduce any part that was not introduced in the description.

The manner of using the paper-laminated closure to seal a plastic bag is identical to that for closures in present use. Namely, one first twists the neck of a bag (not shown here but shown in Fig. 12 of my above patent) into a narrow, cylindrical configuration. Next, holding the closure so that the plane of its base is generally perpendicular to the axis of the neck and so that lead-in notch 12 is adjacent to the neck, one inserts the twisted neck into the lead-in notch until it is forced past gripping points 16 at the base of the notch and into hole 14.

To remove the closure, one first bends it along its horizontal axis (Fig. 1C—an end view—and Figs. 7 and 8) so that the closure is still in contact with the neck of the bag and so that gripping points 16 roughly point in parallel directions. Then one pulls the closure up or down and away from the neck in a direction generally opposite to that in which the gripping points now point, thus freeing the closure from the bag without damaging the latter. The presence of one or two grooves 18 or a longitudinal through-hole 26 (Fig. 6L), either of which acts as a hinge, facilitates this process of bending.

The closure can be used to reseal the original bag or to seal another bag many times; one simply bends it flat again prior to reuse.

As shown in Figs. 1C, 7B, and 8B (all end views), when the closure is bent along its longitudinal axis, region 30 of the base will stretch somewhat along the direction perpendicular to the longitudinal axis. (Region 30 is the region that is parallel to this axis and is on the side of the base opposite to the bend.) Therefore, when the closure is flattened again, the base will have elongated in the direction perpendicular to the longitudinal axis. This will cause a necking down 28 (Figs. 1D, 7C, and 8C) of the base, as well as either a telltale tear 22, or at least a crease 32 (Figs. 7A and 8A) along the axis of bending. Therefore, if the closure is attached to a sales item by a dishonest consumer from the first item to another it will be made evident by the tear or crease.

Figs. 7A and 8A show bent closures with and without grooves, respectively. Figs. 7C and 8C show the same closures, respectively, after being flattened out, along their longitudinal axes, paper tear 22 being visible.

Conclusion, ramifications, and scope. The end of the operation section of the specification often provides a conclusion, summing up, listing any additional ramifications that are not important enough to show in the drawing, and pointing the reader toward the patent claims.

The reader will see that the paper-laminated closure of one or more embodiments can be used to seal a plastic bag easily and conveniently. It can be removed just as easily and without damage to the bag. It can also be used to reseal the bag without requiring a new closure. In addition, when a closure has been used to seal a bag and is later bent and removed so as not to damage the bag, a tear or crease will appear in the paper lamination. This will create visible evidence of tampering without impairing the ability of the closure to reseal the original bag or any other bag. Furthermore, the paper lamination has the additional advantages in that:

(a) it permits the production of closures in a variety of colors without requiring the manufacturer to use a separate facility for the compounding of the powdered or liquid pigments needed for production

(b) it permits an immediate change in the color of the closure being produced without the need for purging the extruder of old resin

(c) it allows the closure to be brightly colored without the need to pigment the base itself and consequently sacrifice the flexibility of the closure. It also allows the closure to be multicolored because the paper lamination offers a perfect surface upon which can be printed multicolored designs

(d) it provides a closure with a superior surface upon which one can label or print

(e) it provides a closure whose labeling cannot be altered or erased without resulting in tell-tale damage to the paper lamination

(f) it provides a closure which will not be slippery when handled with wet or greasy fingers. The paper itself provides a nonslip surface.

Although the description above contains many specificities, these should not be some of the presently preferred embodiments. For example, the closure can have other shapes, such as circular, oval, trapezoidal, triangular, etc.; the lead-in notch can have other shapes; the groove can be replaced by a hinge that connects two otherwise unconnected halves, etc.

Thus the scope should be determined by the appended claims and their legal equivalents, rather than by the examples given.

Computer program. Computer programs having less than 60 lines may be provided in the Detailed Description. Those having from 60 to 300 lines may be provided in the drawing or here. If the program has more than 300 lines, it must be provided on a compact disc. If you are filing the application online using the PTO's EFS-Web system, you may file the listing as an ASCII document in PDF format.

Sequence Listing

If a biotech invention includes a sequence listing of a nucleotide or amino acid sequence, the applicant attaches this information on separate sheets of paper and references the sequence listing in the application (see PTO Rule 77). If there is no sequence listing, the applicant can omit this section or state, "nonapplicable."

Claims

Patent claims establish the boundaries or scope of an invention. They are the standard by which patent rights are measured. In other words, when a patent owner sues for infringement it is because someone has made, used, or sold an invention that has all of the elements in one of the claims, or that closely fits the description in the claims. In this manner, claims function like the boundaries in a deed for real estate. The claims are subject to rigorous examination during patent prosecution (the process of applying for a patent; see Chapter 6).

Claim Language

The patent claims must be specific enough to distinguish the invention from prior art. They must also be clear, logical, and precise. (See 35 U.S.C. § 112(2).) Nonetheless, claims are often the hardest part of the patent to decipher. One reason is that claims follow strict grammatical requirements: They are sentence fragments, always start with an initial capital letter, and contain one period and no quotation marks or parentheses, except in mathematical or chemical formulas. The claims also contain obtuse terminology. To provide an idea of claims drafting, examples of claims for some common inventions and processes are provided below:

Claim for an Automobile:

A self-propelled vehicle, comprising:

    (a) a body carriage having rotatable wheels mounted thereunder for enabling said body carriage to roll along a surface

    (b) *an engine mounted in said carriage for producing rotational energy, and*

    (c) *means for controllably coupling rotational energy from said engine to at least one of said wheels,*

whereby said carriage can be self-propelled along said surface.

Claim for the Process of Sewing:

A method for joining two pieces of cloth together at their edges, comprising the steps of:

    (a) *providing said two pieces of cloth and positioning them together so that an edge portion of one piece overlaps an adjacent edge portion of the other piece, and*

    (b) *passing a thread repeatedly through and along the length of the overlapping portions in sequentially opposite directions and through sequentially spaced holes in said overlapping adjacent portions,*

whereby said two pieces of cloth will be attached along said edge portions.

Claim for Concrete:

A rigid building and paving material comprising a mixture of:

    (a) *sand and stones, and*

    (b) *a hardened cement binder filling the interstices between and adhering to sand and stones,*

whereby a hardened, rigid, and strong matrix for building and paving will be provided.

Claim for a Pencil:

A hand-held writing instrument comprising:

    (a) *elongated core-element means that will leave a marking line if moved across paper or other similar surface, and*

    (b) *an elongated holder surrounding and encasing said elongated core-element means, one portion of said holder being removable from an end thereof to expose an end of said core-element means so as to enable said core-element means to be exposed for writing,*

whereby said holder protects said core-element means from breakage and provides an enlarged means for holding said core-element means conveniently.

Claim for the "Insert" Feature of Word Processing:

A method of inserting additional characters within an existing series of characters on a display, comprising:

    (a) providing a memory that is able to store a series of characters at an adjacent series of addresses in said memory

    (b) providing a character input means that a human operator can use to store a series of characters in said memory at said respective adjacent series of addresses

    (c) storing said series of characters in said memory at said adjacent series of addresses

    (d) providing a display that is operatively connected to said memory for displaying said series of characters stored in said memory at said adjacent series of addresses

    (e) providing a pointer means that said operator can manipulate to point to any location between any adjacent characters within said series of characters displayed on said display, and

    (f) providing a memory controller that will

        (1) direct any additional character that said operator enters via said character input means to a location in said memory, beginning at an address corresponding to the location between said adjacent characters as displayed on said display, and

        (2) cause all characters in said series of characters that are stored in said memory at addresses subsequent said location in said memory to be transferred to subsequent addresses in said memory so that said additional character will be stored in said memory at said location and before all of said subsequent characters,

whereby said display will display said additional character within said series of characters at said location between said adjacent characters, and whereby a writer can add words within existing body of text and the added words are displayed in an orderly and clean fashion without having to reenter said existing body of text.

In addition to Section 112, rules regarding the drafting of claims are provided in the PTO's "Rules of Practice." (PTO Rule 75, parts (b), (d)(1), and (e).)

Defining Common Terms

The following terms and their meanings may prove helpful in deciphering the arcane language of patent claims.

A. Used to introduce a part.

About. Used when the applicant cannot provide a specific quantity: "The thread engagement is undone by rotating the lid unit *about* 90 degrees from the tightened position."

At least. Used to hammer home that more elements can be used.

Contiguous. Used to indicate elements are touching: "Each slide-preventing stop has an upper end surface that is *contiguous* to one side edge of the upper end surface."

Device for. Interpreted as "means for:" "It is an expandable *device for* use in blood vessels and tracts in the body and tension application device for use therewith and method."

Disposed. Used to indicate a part is positioned in a particular place: "A snap-action spring member is *disposed* in a cut portion formed in the outer lid."

Further including. Used in dependent claims to add additional parts: "… said lid unit *further including* a generally L-shaped spring member."

Heretofore. Used to refer back to something previously recited: "There have *heretofore* been strong user demands that such an indication should be provided on the top of the lid."

Indicium. Singular for indices; used to recite something that a human can recognize, such as a mark or a sound: " … so as to provide a field gradient operative to provide an *indicium* of the linear position of the shuttle."

Means for. Used to claim something broadly in terms of its function, rather than specific hardware: "It is an additional object of the invention to provide a compact *means for* pumping a medicament."

Member. Used to recite a mechanical part when no other word is available: " … attached at one end to a drive *member* and at the other end to a fixed point on the base of the pump."

Multitude. Used to recite a large, indefinite number: "In addition, the programming time itself increases to accommodate the *multitude* of different programming thresholds."

Perimeter. Used with its variants (perimetric, etc.) to refer to a border around something.

Pivotably or pivotally. Used to indicate that a part is rotatably mounted: "The blade is *pivotably* carried at one of its ends around a support shaft."

Plurality. Used to introduce more than one of an element: " … a ROM memory having a *plurality* of reference potential transmission lines."

Predetermined. Used to state that a part has a specific parameter: "Programming stops when the gate threshold voltage has reached a certain *predetermined* point."

Providing. Used to recite a part in a method claim: "Oxide-nitride-oxide layers are formed above the channel area and between the bit lines for *providing* isolation between overlying silicon layers."

Releasably. Something can be released from a position.

Respectively. Used to relate several parts to several other parts in an individual manner: "A left and a right bit are stored in physically different areas of the charge trapping layer, near left and right regions of the memory cell, *respectively*."

Said. Used to refer to a previously recited part by the same word: " … *said* memory cell having a first region and a second region with a channel there between and having a gate above said channel."

Sandwiching. Used to indicate that one part is between two other parts: "Further, the thinner top and bottom oxide *sandwiching* the nitride layer helps in retention of the trapped charge."

Selected from the group consisting of. Used in a *Markush* claim to create an artificial group.

Slidably. Used to indicate that two parts slide with respect to each other: "The charging roller bearing is *slidably* fitted in a guide groove."

So that. Used to restrict a part to a defined function: "The cup holders are usually provided with annular grooves or vertical flutes *so that* the holder is only in contact with the cup."

So that or such that. Used to restrict a part to a defined function: "These grooves or flutes provide a structural integrity to the cup holders *such that* they must be packaged in substantially the same form as they will be used."

Substantially. Used to fudge a specific recitation: "The side plate which has the hole is also provided with a toner filling opening *substantially* shaped like a right triangle."

Surrounding. Used to indicate that a part is surrounded: "The elastic sealing members exactly cover the corresponding lengthwise end portions of the flange *surrounding* the recessed surface."

The. Used to refer to a previously recited part by a slightly different word.

Thereby. Used to specify a result or connection between an element and what it doe: "Said sleeping bag is supported by said carrying straps and carried *thereby* on one's back."

Thereof. Used as a pronoun to avoid repeating a part name. "Said back wall each being padded and being of equal width, being joined at the sides and the bottom *thereof*."

Urging. Used to indicate that force is exacted upon a part: "By pressing the rod against the *urging* of the spring, the link members straighten out."

Whereby. Used to introduce a function or result at the end of a claim:"*Whereby* the handle portion attaches to the handle of the device by the securing mechanisms."

Wherein. Used in a dependent claim to recite an element (part) more specifically: "A portable printing device as claimed in claim 13, *wherein* the shutter member includes … "

Independent and Dependent Claims

The claims of a patent usually contain several sets of claims; each set usually consists of an independent claim and several dependent claims. The independent claim of one set is usually drafted as broadly as possible and then followed successively with narrower dependent claims designed to specifically recite possible specific aspects or additional features. Each dependent claim can refer back to the independent claim directly or indirectly by referring to an intermediate dependent claim, which refers back to the independent claim or to another intermediate dependent claim. Each independent claim stands by itself while a dependent claim always refers back and incorporates the language of another independent or dependent claim. (See 35 U.S.C. § 112(3) and (4).) Below is an example of an independent claim and a dependent claim for a golf club and bag security system (Pat. No. 5,973,596). In this example, the independent claim defines the elements of the golf bag security system and the dependent claim recites one aspect of it more specifically by stating that the alarm can be turned on and off by a separate device.

Independent Claim

    1. A golf bag security system for detecting movement of at least one golf club in a golf bag, the golf bag security system comprising:

      a. a detection loop substantially arranged around the circumference of a golf bag

      b. a loop oscillator circuit, connected to the detection loop

      c. a control circuit, capable of detecting a change in inductance in the loop, identifying an alarm condition in response to the change of inductance, and

      d. an alarm device responsive to the alarm condition.

Dependent Claim

    2. The system defined in claim 1, further including an arming device enabling or disabling the security system. This claim is interpreted as if all of the language of claim 1 were incorporated; it does not cover the arming device per se.

Reading Patent Claims for Infringement

In a patent infringement lawsuit, the plaintiff (patent owner) will ask the judge to examine the claims of the patented invention, and then compare them to the defendant's device or process, to determine if the claims "read on" (or cover) the defendant's device or process. To infringe a patent, the defendant's device must physically have or perform all of the elements contained in one of the claims. For example, if a patent claim recites two elements, (1) a hidden pocket in a scarf, and (2) a snap that makes the pocket closeable, a device that contains only a hidden pocket without a snap in a scarf won't infringe.

A dependent claim cannot be infringed unless the allegedly infringing invention also infringes the related independent claim. In other words, if an independent claim is not infringed, then the dependent claims cannot be infringed.

Abstract

Although introduced relatively recently, the most widely read portion of the patent is the abstract. The abstract is a concise, one-paragraph summary (150 words maximum) of the structure, nature, and purpose of the entire disclosure. The abstract is used by the PTO and the public to quickly determine the gist of what is being disclosed. The abstract is a condensed version of the specification. Below are examples of two abstracts.

Abstract for Doll Carrier (Pat. No. 5,803,331. See Fig. 5B, below)

ABSTRACT: A carrier for doll-type toys is provided having a pocket-like enclosure for carrying the doll-type toy in a partially displayed position. The enclosure includes a double-wall section forming an envelope or bag, in which the doll-type toy is carried, and a single-wall section, against which the doll-type toy is partially displayed. This single-wall section extends beyond and above the double walled section. Carrying straps permit the enclosure to be carried on the back of a child in backpack fashion. The carrying straps are attached adjacent to the free end of the single-wall section and at the side of the double-wall section. A second and smaller pocket enclosure may be attached to the front face of the carrier.

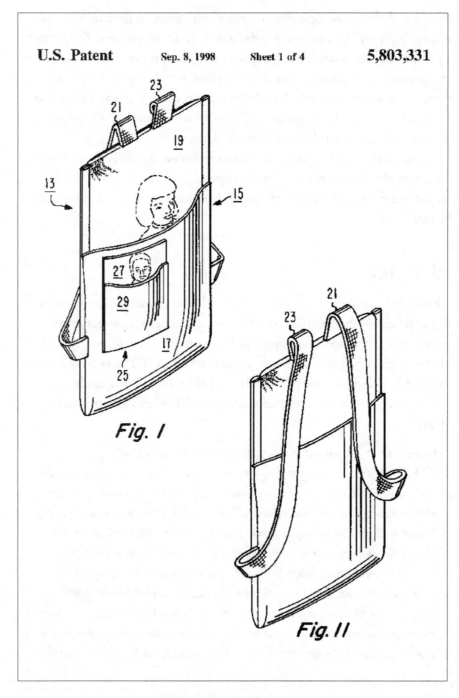

Figure 5B—Doll Carrier

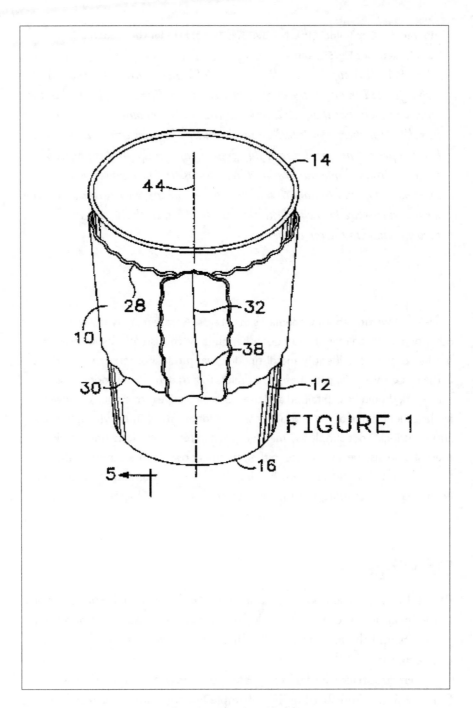

Figure 5C—Cup Holder

Abstract for Cup holder (Pat. No. 5,425,497—Sold Under the Trademark "Java Jacket." See Fig. 5C, above)

ABSTRACT: A cup holder is in the form of a sheet with distal ends. A web is formed in one of the ends, and a corresponding slot is formed in the other end such that the ends interlock. Thus the cup holder is assembled by rolling the sheet and interlocking the ends. The sheet can be an elongate band of pressed material, preferably pressed paper pulp, and is preferably formed with multiple nubbins and depressions. In one embodiment, the sheet has a top and bottom that are accurate and concentric, and matching webs and cuts are formed in each end of the sheet, with the cuts being perpendicular to the top of the sheet.

TIP

Writing about trademarks in patents. A trademark is any word or other symbol that a manufacturer or other business consistently associates with a product or service to identify and distinguish that product or service from others in the marketplace. If a patent applicant refers to a trademarked product, the trademark should be capitalized and used as an adjective (not a noun), followed by the generic name of the product or service, for example, *"The Club* automobile anti-theft lock" (not simply as "*The Club*"). When referring to the trademark, there should also be a reference to the trademark owner, for example, "'*The Club*' automobile anti-theft lock distributed by Winner International of Sharon, Pennsylvania." (For more information on trademarks, see Chapter 1.)

Drawings

Patent drawings (also known as "drawing sheets") are visual representations of the invention and must be included with the application, if necessary to understand the patent. The drawings must show every feature recited in the claims.

There are strict standards for patent drawings as to materials, size, form, symbols, and shading. For example, writing is not permitted in the margins and there can be no holes punched in the drawing sheet.

A patent applicant has two choices when filing a patent: The application can include formal or informal drawings. However, the application will not be examined until formal drawings are filed (Rule 85).

Formal drawings are usually CAD drawings or other computer-created drawings, or copies of ink drawings done with instruments on Bristol board or Mylar film and in accordance with PTO rules. Informal drawings are usually photocopies of good pencil or ink sketches that include all the details of the invention.

If an applicant wants to file abroad, formal drawings will usually have to be filed with the foreign application within 12 months after the patent application is filed. Also, if the PTO doesn't require them earlier, formal drawings must be filed after the U.S. patent is allowed. For more information about patent drawing requirements, read *How to Make Patent Drawings*, by Patent Agent Jack Lo and Attorney David Pressman (Nolo), and see 35 U.S.C. § 113 and 37 CFR §§ 1.53 and 1.84.

The applicant may no longer use black-and-white photos for patent drawings unless a photo is necessary to show the invention—for example, fine structures such as a granular composition. Color photos or color drawings may also be used if necessary to illustrate the invention properly. In that case, an applicant must file three sets of color photos or drawings. A statement must be included in the specification referencing the colored drawings, and a petition explaining why color is necessary, along with a fee, must be filed. All drawings must be submitted in either 8.5 x 11-inch size (U.S. standard) or 210 mm x 297 mm size (A4 international standard).

Preparation of a Patent Application

In this section, we provide basic information about a patent application. For detailed information on preparing a patent application, read *Patent It Yourself*, by patent attorney David E. Blau and patent agent David Pressman (Nolo).

The preparation of a patent application requires assembling a group of documents according to PTO rules. Below is a table of documents used for patent application preparation.

Specification (Including Description, Claims, and Abstract) and Drawings

These documents make up the substance of the patent application and are discussed in detail in the previous sections of this chapter.

Information Disclosure Statement

The PTO rules impose on each patent applicant a "duty of candor and good faith." This means that all applicants and their attorneys must disclose information about prior art they are aware of that might influence the patent examiner in deciding on the application. The Information Disclosure Statement (IDS) is used to comply with this candor requirement. All applicants must submit an IDS at the time of applying, within the following three months, or before the first Office Action. (For information on Office Actions, see Chapter 6.) The IDS consists of a transmittal letter (not necessary if the application is filed electronically) and a PTO Form SB/08, on which prior art is listed. Examples of the forms are shown in Figs. 5D and 5E, below. An applicant who is not aware of any relevant prior art does not have to file an IDS. An applicant who later becomes aware of relevant prior art must disclose it by a later IDS. A fee must be paid if the IDS is filed after the first Office Action.

The applicant must also include with the IDS a copy of each cited foreign or nonpatent literature reference (U.S. patents and published patent applications need not be included) and a discussion of the relevance of any non-English language references to the invention. In other words, copies of articles and non-U.S. patent publications must be attached.

Documents Used for Patent Application Preparation	
Specification	Required
Claims	Required
Abstract	Required
Drawings	Required if necessary to understand the invention
Information Disclosure Statement	Required if applicant knows of any relevant prior art, but can be filed within three months of application
Patent Application Declaration	Required
Petition to Make Special Because of Age or Poor Health	Optional and can be filed at any time
Petition to Make Special under the Accelerated Examination Program	Must be filed at the time of filing if a search has been made (the requirements of the filing are demanding and complex)
Assignment and Cover Sheet	Required if an inventor is transferring ownership of patent; can be filed at any time
Return Receipt Postcard (optional)	Optional, but desirable if paper patent application is filed
Filing Fee (check or Credit Card Payment Form)	Required
Transmittal Letter	Required if filing a paper application (not required if filing electronically via the EFS system)*
Fee Transmittal	Required if filing a paper application (not required if filing electronically via the EFS system)*

*Although not strictly required, the transmittal letter and fee transmittal are usually included. For more information on the technical details regarding transmittal letters and fee transmittals, review PTO Rules at the PTO website, www.uspto.gov.

In the United States Patent and Trademark Office

Serial Number: _____

Appn. Filed: _____

Applicant(s): _____

Appn. Title: _____

Examiner/GAU: _____

Mailed: _____

At: _____

Information Disclosure Statement Cover Letter

Commissioner for Patents
P.O. Box 1450
Alexandria, VA 22313-1450

Sir:

Attached is a completed Form PTO/SB/08(A&B) and copies of any non-U.S. patent references cited thereon. Following are comments on any non-English-language references pursuant to Rule 98:

Very respectfully,

Applicant(s): _____

_____

Enc.: PTO/SB/08(A&B)

c/o: _____

_____

_____

Telephone: _____

Certificate of Mailing

I certify that this correspondence will be deposited with the United States Postal Service as first-class mail with proper postage affixed in an envelope addressed to: "Commissioner for Patents, P.O. Box 1450, Alexandria, VA 22313-1450" on the date below.

Date: 20_____   _____, Applicant

Figure 5D—Information Disclosure Statement

PTO/SB/08a (07-09)
Approved for use through 11/30/2020. OMB 0651-0031
U.S. Patent and Trademark Office; U.S. DEPARTMENT OF COMMERCE
Under the Paperwork Reduction Act of 1995, no persons are required to respond to a collection of information unless it contains a valid OMB control number.

Substitute for form 1449/PTO

INFORMATION DISCLOSURE STATEMENT BY APPLICANT

(Use as many sheets as necessary)

Sheet _____ of _____

Complete if Known

Application Number	
Filing Date	
First Named Inventor	
Art Unit	
Examiner Name	
Attorney Docket Number	

U. S. PATENT DOCUMENTS

Examiner Initials*	Cite No.[1]	Document Number Number-Kind Code[2] *(if known)*	Publication Date MM-DD-YYYY	Name of Patentee or Applicant of Cited Document	Pages, Columns, Lines, Where Relevant Passages or Relevant Figures Appear
		US-			
		US-			
		US-			
		US-			
		US-			
		US-			
		US-			
		US-			
		US-			
		US-			
		US-			
		US-			
		US-			
		US-			
		US-			
		US-			
		US-			
		US-			
		US-			

FOREIGN PATENT DOCUMENTS

Examiner Initials*	Cite No.[1]	Foreign Patent Document Country Code[3] Number[4] Kind Code[5] *(if known)*	Publication Date MM-DD-YYYY	Name of Patentee or Applicant of Cited Document	Pages, Columns, Lines, Where Relevant Passages Or Relevant Figures Appear	T[6]

Examiner Signature		Date Considered	

*EXAMINER: Initial if reference considered, whether or not citation is in conformance with MPEP 609. Draw line through citation if not in conformance and not considered. Include copy of this form with next communication to applicant. [1] Applicant's unique citation designation number (optional). [2] See Kinds Codes of USPTO Patent Documents at www.uspto.gov or MPEP 901.04. [3] Enter Office that issued the document, by the two-letter code (WIPO Standard ST.3). [4] For Japanese patent documents, the indication of the year of the reign of the Emperor must precede the serial number of the patent document. [5] Kind of document by the appropriate symbols as indicated on the document under WIPO Standard ST.16 if possible. [6] Applicant is to place a check mark here if English language Translation is attached.

This collection of information is required by 37 CFR 1.97 and 1.98. The information is required to obtain or retain a benefit by the public which is to file (and by the USPTO to process) an application. Confidentiality is governed by 35 U.S.C. 122 and 37 CFR 1.14. This collection is estimated to take 2 hours to complete, including gathering, preparing, and submitting the completed application form to the USPTO. Time will vary depending upon the individual case. Any comments on the amount of time you require to complete this form and/or suggestions for reducing this burden, should be sent to the Chief Information Officer, U.S. Patent and Trademark Office, P.O. Box 1450, Alexandria, VA 22313-1450. DO NOT SEND FEES OR COMPLETED FORMS TO THIS ADDRESS. **SEND TO: Commissioner for Patents, P.O. Box 1450, Alexandria, VA 22313-1450.**

If you need assistance in completing the form, call 1-800-PTO-9199 (1-800-786-9199) and select option 2.

Figure 5E—PTO Form SB/08

PTO/AIA/01 (06-12)
Approved for use through 01/31/2014. OMB 0651-0032
U.S. Patent and Trademark Office; U.S. DEPARTMENT OF COMMERCE
Under the Paperwork Reduction Act of 1995, no persons are required to respond to a collection of information unless it displays a valid OMB control number.

DECLARATION (37 CFR 1.63) FOR UTILITY OR DESIGN APPLICATION USING AN APPLICATION DATA SHEET (37 CFR 1.76)

Title of Invention	

As the below named inventor, I hereby declare that:

This declaration is directed to:

☐ The attached application, or

☐ United States application or PCT international application number _____

filed on _____.

The above-identified application was made or authorized to be made by me.

I believe that I am the original inventor or an original joint inventor of a claimed invention in the application.

I hereby acknowledge that any willful false statement made in this declaration is punishable under 18 U.S.C. 1001 by fine or imprisonment of not more than five (5) years, or both.

WARNING:

Petitioner/applicant is cautioned to avoid submitting personal information in documents filed in a patent application that may contribute to identity theft. Personal information such as social security numbers, bank account numbers, or credit card numbers (other than a check or credit card authorization form PTO-2038 submitted for payment purposes) is never required by the USPTO to support a petition or an application. If this type of personal information is included in documents submitted to the USPTO, petitioners/applicants should consider redacting such personal information from the documents before submitting them to the USPTO. Petitioner/applicant is advised that the record of a patent application is available to the public after publication of the application (unless a non-publication request in compliance with 37 CFR 1.213(a) is made in the application) or issuance of a patent. Furthermore, the record from an abandoned application may also be available to the public if the application is referenced in a published application or an issued patent (see 37 CFR 1.14). Checks and credit card authorization forms PTO-2038 submitted for payment purposes are not retained in the application file and therefore are not publicly available.

LEGAL NAME OF INVENTOR

Inventor: _____   Date (Optional) :_____

Signature: _____

Note: An application data sheet (PTO/SB/14 or equivalent), including naming the entire inventive entity, must accompany this form or must have been previously filed. Use an additional PTO/AIA/01 form for each additional inventor.

This collection of information is required by 35 U.S.C. 115 and 37 CFR 1.63. The information is required to obtain or retain a benefit by the public which is to file (and by the USPTO to process) an application. Confidentiality is governed by 35 U.S.C. 122 and 37 CFR 1.11 and 1.14. This collection is estimated to take 1 minute to complete, including gathering, preparing, and submitting the completed application form to the USPTO. Time will vary depending upon the individual case. Any comments on the amount of time you require to complete this form and/or suggestions for reducing this burden, should be sent to the Chief Information Officer, U.S. Patent and Trademark Office, U.S. Department of Commerce, P.O. Box 1450, Alexandria, VA 22313-1450. DO NOT SEND FEES OR COMPLETED FORMS TO THIS ADDRESS. **SEND TO: Commissioner for Patents, P.O. Box 1450, Alexandria, VA 22313-1450.**
If you need assistance in completing the form, call 1-800-PTO-9199 and select option 2.

Figure 5F—Patent Application Declaration

Patent Application Declaration (PAD)

The declaration identifies the inventor or joint inventors and provides a statement by the applicant that the inventor understands the contents of the claims and specification and has fully disclosed all material information. The PTO provides a form for the declaration (see Fig. 5F). (For more information, see 35 U.S.C. § 115 and 37 CFR §§ 1.51–1.68.)

Power of Attorney

Only an inventor, a patent agent, or a patent attorney may prepare and file a patent application. If an attorney or agent is preparing an application on behalf of an inventor, a power of attorney (Form PTO/SB/80 covers agents as well as attorneys) is usually executed to formally authorize the patent attorney or agent to act on behalf of the inventor. The power of attorney form was previously part of the PAD but is now filed as a separate document. If the rights to the patent have been assigned and the assignment has been recorded, the assignee can execute the power of attorney. If the inventor is preparing and filing the application "pro se" (without an attorney), then a power of attorney is not filed. Licensed patent attorneys and agents may also represent patent applicants without a power of attorney. (37 CFR § 1.34.)

Reduced Fees for Small and Micro Entities

In order to encourage inventors from diverse economic backgrounds, fees are reduced for small businesses, independent inventors, and nonprofit companies. The patent laws provide three sets of fees: (1) regular or large-entity fees for large companies (more than 500 employees); (2) small-entity fees for independent inventors who make more than about $206,109 per year or who have been named as an inventor in more than four patent applications, and who have no obligation to assign the invention to a large entity, a small business (less than 500 employees), or a nonprofit company; and (3) micro-entity fees for independent inventors who make less than about $206,109 per year and have not been named as an inventor in more than four patent applications, or who qualify as a small entity and who work for or who have an obligation to assign the invention to an institution of higher learning. The small-entity fees are half of the large-entity fees and the micro-entity fees are half of the small-entity fees. An independent inventor must either own all rights, or have transferred—or be obligated to transfer—rights to a small business or nonprofit organization. Nonprofit organizations are defined and listed in the Code of Federal Regulations and usually are educational institutions or charitable organizations.

If the inventor qualifies as a small entity, a Small Entity Declaration is no longer required. The inventor simply indicates that he or she is entitled to small-entity status on the Fee Transmittal and pays the small-entity fee. Small-entity status is lost if patent rights are transferred—or obligated to be transferred—to an entity that does not qualify as a small entity. In that case, the inventor is obligated to tell the PTO that small-entity status is no longer appropriate and the inventor must pay large-entity fees after that.

However, if the inventor qualifies as a micro entity, a Micro Entity Declaration is required. The PTO has two Micro Entity Declarations: One (SB-15A) requires inventors to state that their previous year's income was below a given amount, and that the number of patent applications that the inventor has filed in their lifetime is not more than four. The other declaration (SB-15B) requires inventors to state that the application is owned by an institution of higher education. Once either type of Micro Entity Declaration is filed, the inventor can pay micro- entity fees throughout the entire life of the patent application. But micro-entity status is lost if patent rights are transferred —or obligated to be transferred—to an entity that does not qualify as a small entity or if the inventor no longer qualifies because of income or the number of patent applications filed. In that case the inventor is obligated to tell the PTO that micro-entity status is no longer appropriate and the inventor must pay small-entity fees after that.

Petition to Make Special

There are three basic ways to get your examination expedited: (A) by filing a simple "Petition to Make Special" (PTMS) based on either (1) old age or health, (2)(i) environmental enhancement, (ii) conservation of energy, or (iii) countering terrorism; (B) by filing a more complicated PTMS under the Accelerated Examination Program (AEP); and (C) by buying a prioritized examination under the AIA.

Unless you have a specific need for the early examination or issuance of a patent—for example, an infringement is occurring and you need a patent to get capital for manufacturing the invention, or the technology is rapidly becoming obsolete, or you're contemplating foreign filing—most patent professionals agree that there is usually little to be gained in filing a PTMS or buying a prioritized examination. The AEP program is discussed in more detail below. The fee for buying a prioritized examination is steep: $4,200 for a large entity, $2,100 for a small entity, and $1,050 for a micro entity.

The Accelerated Examination Program (AEP)

In the above three ways to expedite examination of a patent application, Types A (simple PTMS) and C (buying a prioritized examination) are easy to implement. Type A merely requires a simple petition and is free, and Type C is like Type A except that it requires a high fee. The second way, Type B (the AEP), was introduced in 2007. Unfortunately, it is complex and time consuming. Under this procedure, the USPTO will advance an application for examination out of turn if the applicant files a grantable Petition to Make Special. It must be filed electronically using EFS-Web and Form SB28 at the same time.

The applicant must (1) make a search, then prepare an Information Disclosure Statement (IDS) citing the references in the search, and then (2) identify the limitations of the claims that are disclosed in the references, how the claims are patentable over the references, discuss the utility of the invention, list references that may be disqualified as references because they came from the same organization (see 35 U.S.C. § 103(c)), state where each limitation of the claims finds support in the specification, detail the search that was made, including where it was made, and state the reason for accelerated examination. The application may not include more than three independent and 20 total claims, and must claim one invention only. As you can see, the rules are very detailed and appear to be designed to make the process more difficult to navigate. For more information, see the Notice in the *Official Gazette* of 2006 July 18. The PTO has provided samples of the Request for Expedited Examination (www.uspto.gov/patents/initiatives/accelerated-examination). Some practitioners have stated that, given all the work required to participate in the AEP, it is cheaper to buy a prioritized examination if one is using an attorney.

Assignment

Before passage of the America Invents Act (AIA) in September 2011, a patent application had to be filed in the name of the true inventor or inventors. The AIA modified that to permit a person to whom an inventor has assigned (or is under an obligation to assign) an invention to make an application for the patent, as well, provided that filing by the assignee is necessary to preserve the rights of the parties. If there is more than one inventor, each becomes an applicant for the patent and each automatically owns equal shares of the invention and any patents that may issue. (For more information about patent ownership, see Chapter 7.)

Inventorship can be different from ownership. Often all or part of the ownership of the invention and the patent application must be transferred to someone else or some business entity. For example, the inventor may work for a company and as a condition of employment, has agreed to transfer ownership of inventions. To make the transfer, the inventor must legally transfer the interest by assignment and the assignment must also be filed either with the patent application or at any time afterward.

If an assignment of a patent application has been recorded and the applicant refers to that fact in the issue fee transmittal form, the PTO will print the patent with the assignee's interest indicated. For example, an egg storage device patent was assigned and the inventor and assignee were listed as follows:

INVENTOR: Onneweer, Frederik J., Tervuren, Belgium

ASSIGNEE AT ISSUE: Dart Industries Inc., Deerfield, Illinois

Even if the patent doesn't indicate the assignment, the assignment will still be effective if the PTO has recorded it. The PTO requires that all assignments submitted for recording be accompanied by a cover letter.

Filing by Mail

The following three sections cover filing a patent application by mail. We strongly recommend filing electronically, and not filing by mail because there is a $400 surcharge for a large entity or a $200 surcharge for a small entity or a micro entity for filing a paper application by mail. Also, filing electronically will save the Priority Mail Express fee and provide an instant acknowledgment of filing, together with the serial number and filing date of the application.

Return Receipt Postcard

Because it often takes weeks for the PTO to officially acknowledge receipt of an application or any other paper, the only way to quickly verify receipt is to enclose a stamped return postcard with the mailed materials. The back of the card contains the inventor's name, title of invention, number of pages of specification, claims, abstract, the date the Patent Application Declaration was signed, the number of sheets of drawing (and whether formal or informal), and the check number and amount. The applicant usually receives the postcard back from the PTO within two to four weeks of filing the application. If an application is filed electronically (online), of course no postcard is needed and the PTO will provide an instant acknowledgment of the filing.

Check, Money Order, or Credit Card Payment for Correct Filing Fee

The applicant must enclose the appropriate fee, a Fee Transmittal Letter (see Fig. 5G, below) and a Credit Card Payment Form (if paying by credit card). The fee depends on several variables, including the number of independent and dependent claims, whether the applicant qualifies for Small Entity or Micro Entity Status, and whether an assignment is being filed. Payment can be made by personal check or money order made out to the Commissioner for Patents for the total amount, and should be attached to the transmittal letter. An applicant paying by credit card should use the PTO's Credit Card Payment Form (PTO Form 2038) with the Fee Transmittal Letter. The PTO does not accept debit cards or check cards requiring a personal identification number (PIN). If an application is filed electronically (online) the online forms contain a place to enter the credit card information.

Transmittal Letter

The transmittal letter is the cover letter that details what is being filed, the names of inventors, the number of pages, the fee, and other information used by the PTO to categorize the filing (see Fig. 5H, below). If the applicant previously filed a provisional patent application, that information should also be listed. The transmittal letter also permits an inventor to ask the examiner to write allowable claims for the invention. (See MPEP § 707.07(j).) All of the inventors must sign the transmittal letter. The entire package of application materials is mailed to: Commissioner for Patents, P.O. Box 1450, Alexandria, VA 22313-1450. In Chapter 6, we discuss what happens at the PTO after the application is filed. If an application is filed electronically (online), the online forms contain the equivalent of a transmittal letter.

Inventors can use form PTO-2038 to pay fees by credit card. The form can be downloaded from the PTO website.

All patent applications are now published 18 months after filing unless at the time of filing, the inventor files a Non-Publication Request (NPR; PTO Form SB/35), stating that the application will not be filed outside the United States. If the application is filed via the Internet or on paper, it is very desirable to file an Application Data Sheet (ADS; PTO Form SB/14) listing all necessary data about the applicant and the application; the ADS contains an NPR. If an inventor does not request nonpublication the application will be published after 18 months and the inventor will be charged $300 more when the application is allowed. If an inventor requests nonpublication and subsequently files a foreign application, he or she must rescind the NPR within 45 days and authorize publication.

Electronic Filing (The EFS System)

The PTO has an online filing system that enables applicants to file patent applications and provisional patent applications via the Internet. The PTO's Electronic Filing System (EFS) assembles application components (including figures), calculates fees, and transmits the completed application to the PTO via a digitally encrypted secure system.

EFS Advantages

The PTO's Electronic Filing System using the Internet (EFS-Web) enables patent applications, amendments, and other documents to be filed electronically over the Internet. However, it requires some time to master. Previously, all documents had to be converted to the Portable Data Format (PDF) but now they can be filed in Microsoft Word. The advantages of electronic filing are so great that even if you're filing just one application, it is worth the effort. As stated, its advantages are: You can (1) file an application anytime and from anywhere that has Internet access, (2) obtain instant confirmation of receipt of documents by the PTO, (3) send an application to the PTO without having to go to the post office to get a Priority Mail Express receipt, (4) file with confidence because you will get an instant acknowledgment without having to prepare a postcard or wait for a postcard receipt, (5) avoid the paper-filing surcharge—see "Filing by Mail" above, and (6) file an application without having to prepare an application transmittal, a fee transmittal, receipt postcard, or check or Credit Card Payment Form (CCPF).

Become a Registered eFiler (If Time Permits)

If you plan on filing electronically and if you can wait several weeks to file, I recommend you become a registered eFiler. You'll have to deal with red tape, including filling out a form to obtain a customer number, sending a notarized certificate to the PTO, obtaining access codes, and calling the PTO to confirm, but as a registered eFiler you'll be able to track your application's progress and file additional documents or corrections. To register go to the Patent Electronic Business Center on the USPTO website (www.uspto.gov/learning-and-resources/support-centers/patent-electronic-business-center) and follow the detailed instructions. If you can't wait several weeks, you can use EFS-Web to file an application as an unregistered eFiler and register later.

e-Office Actions

The PTO now has an optional "e-Office Action" service whereby they will send all correspondence to up to three of your email addresses in lieu of postal mail. To guard against lost emails, they will send a postcard reminder if the email is not opened within a week. This service can be useful if you're traveling, your mail is unreliable, or you want to get correspondence quickly. If you're a registered eFiler, you can learn more about this service at www.uspto.gov/learning-and-resources/support-centers/electronic-business-center/patent-online-services.

Preparing an Application for EFS

If you're ready to file electronically, take the following steps:

- **Prepare the application as usual.** Before you go online, prepare the entire application as described above, except omit the Application Transmittal form, Fee Transmittal form, Receipt Postcard, and check or CCPF. Sign the declaration as usual.

- **Convert your application to PDF format.** Although conversion of documents to PDF form is no longer necessary, we still recommend you convert all documents of the application (drawings, specification, including any claims and abstract), to PDF documents in your computer since PDF documents are more permanent and harder to alter. All PDF documents submitted via EFS-Web must have a minimum resolution of 300 DPI and a white background.

- **Prepare a PDF data sheet.** Get instructions on completing this form, and find the fillable and savable EFS Application Data Sheet (ADS; PTO Form SB/14) by going to www.uspto.gov/patents/ apply/forms/important-information-completing-application-data-sheet-ads.

- **Sign on.** On the USPTO website, go to the "File Online" page under "Patents" (www.uspto.gov/patents/apply). If you haven't registered as an eFiler, click on "EFS-Web for Unregistered eFilers," fill in your name and email and the type of application. If you have registered, click on "EFS-Web for Registered eFilers" and follow the instructions.

- **Application data.** On the "Application Data" page fill in the title of the invention, a docket number for the application of your choosing, and your name and customer number or address. It's best to copy this data electronically from your Data Sheet so that everything will be consistent.

- **Attach PDF files.** On the "Attach Documents" page click the "Browse" button and find your PDF (or Word) documents.

When you've attached all of the files, click the "Upload &
Validate" button at the bottom.

- **Review documents.** After a few minutes, you'll eventually get
  a Review Documents page, which should show all of the
  documents you've attached. When there are no fatal errors click
  "Continue."

- **Calculate fees.** On the "Calculate Fees" page, select your entity
  size, which will usually be small entity or micro entity. If you are
  eligible to file as a micro entity, you must also file one of the two
  Micro Entity declarations (see above). Check and complete all
  the applicable boxes on the form and then click the "Calculate"
  button. (The search, filing, and examination fees must all be paid
  at once.)

- **Submit application.** This page will list all of your PDF (or Word)
  files, a Fee-Info.pdf file, and the filing fee. If everything is
  okay, click the "Submit" button at the bottom to bring up a
  "Congratulations!" page with an assigned Application Number,
  Confirmation Number, and Total Fees due. Click the "YES!"
  button at the bottom to pay.

- **Review fees and select payment method.** Unless you have a PTO
  Deposit Account or are set up for EFT, select "Charge Credit
  Card," then the "Start online payment process" button to bring
  up the payment page. Fill out the blanks and click the "Confirm"
  button at the bottom.

- **Acknowledgment receipt.** If everything is okay, you'll get an
  Acknowledgment Receipt, which is analogous to the receipt
  postcard used for mailed filings.

If you do file electronically, you will, several weeks after filing,
receive by mail a formal paper filing receipt, unless you opted to receive
e-Office Actions (above).

PTO/SB/17 (10-20)
Approved for use through 12/31/2020. OMB 0651-0032
U.S. Patent and Trademark Office; U.S. DEPARTMENT OF COMMERCE
Under the Paperwork Reduction Act of 1995 no persons are required to respond to a collection of information unless it displays a valid OMB control number

FEE TRANSMITTAL

	Complete if known
Application Number	
Filing Date	
First Named Inventor	
Examiner Name	
Art Unit	
Practitioner Docket No.	

☐ Applicant asserts small entity status. See 37 CFR 1.27.

☐ Applicant certifies micro entity status. See 37 CFR 1.29.
Form PTO/SB/15A or B or equivalent must either be enclosed or have been submitted previously.

TOTAL AMOUNT OF PAYMENT ($) _____

METHOD OF PAYMENT (check all that apply)

☐ Check ☐ Credit Card ☐ Money Order ☐ None ☐ Other (please identify): _____

☐ Deposit Account Deposit Account Number: _____ Deposit Account Name: _____

For the above-identified deposit account, the Director is hereby authorized to (check all that apply):

☐ Charge fee(s) indicated below   ☐ Charge fee(s) indicated below, **except for the filing fee**

☐ Charge any additional fee(s) or underpayment of fee(s)   ☐ Credit any overpayment of fee(s)
under 37 CFR 1.16 and 1.17

WARNING: Information on this form may become public. Credit card information should not be included on this form. Provide credit card information and authorization on PTO-2038.

FEE CALCULATION

1. BASIC FILING, SEARCH, AND EXAMINATION FEES (U = undiscounted fee; S = small entity fee; M = micro entity fee)

	FILING FEES			SEARCH FEES			EXAMINATION FEES			
Application Type	**U ($)**	**S ($)**	**M ($)**	**U ($)**	**S ($)**	**M ($)**	**U ($)**	**S ($)**	**M ($)**	**Fees Paid ($)**
Utility	320	160*	80	700	350	175	800	400	200	_____
Design	220	110	55	160	80	40	640	320	160	_____
Plant	220	110	55	440	220	110	660	330	165	_____
Reissue	320	160	80	700	350	175	2,320	1,160	580	_____
Provisional	300	150	75	0	0	0	0	0	0	_____

* The $160 small entity status filing fee for a utility application is further reduced to $80 for a small entity status applicant who files the application via EFS-Web.

2. EXCESS CLAIM FEES

Fee Description	**Undiscounted Fee ($)**	**Small Entity Fee ($)**	**Micro Entity Fee ($)**
Each claim over 20 (including Reissues)	100	50	25
Each independent claim over 3 (including Reissues)	480	240	120
Multiple dependent claims	860	430	215

Total Claims		**Extra Claims**		**Fee ($)**		**Fee Paid ($)**
_____	-20 or HP =	_____	x	_____	=	_____

HP = highest number of total claims paid for, if greater than 20.

Indep. Claims		**Extra Claims**		**Fee ($)**		**Fee Paid ($)**
_____	-3 or HP =	_____	x	_____	=	_____

Multiple Dependent Claims

Fee ($)	**Fee Paid ($)**
_____	_____

HP = highest number of independent claims paid for, if greater than 3.

3. APPLICATION SIZE FEE

If the specification and drawings exceed 100 sheets of paper (excluding electronically filed sequence or computer listings under 37 CFR 1.52(e)), the application size fee due is $420 ($210 for small entity) ($105 for micro entity) for each additional 50 sheets or fraction thereof. See 35 U.S.C. 41(a)(1)(G) and 37 CFR 1.16(s).

Total Sheets		**Extra Sheets**		**Number of each additional 50 or fraction thereof**		**Fee ($)**		**Fee Paid ($)**
_____	- 100 =	_____	/ 50 =	_____ (round **up** to a whole number)	x	_____	=	_____

4. OTHER FEE(S)

Fees Paid ($)

Non-English specification, $140 fee ($70 for small entity) ($35 for micro entity) _____

Non-electronic filing fee under 37 CFR 1.16(t) for a utility application, $400 fee ($200 small or micro entity) _____

Other (e.g., late filing surcharge): _____ _____

SUBMITTED BY			
Signature		Registration No. (Attorney/Agent)	Telephone
Name (Print/Type)			Date

This collection of information is required by 37 CFR 1.136. The information is required to obtain or retain a benefit by the public which is to file (and by the USPTO to process) an application. Confidentiality is governed by 35 U.S.C. 122 and 37 CFR 1.14. This collection is estimated to take 30 minutes to complete, including gathering, preparing, and submitting the completed application form to the USPTO. Time will vary depending upon the individual case. Any comments on the amount of time you require to complete this form and/or suggestions for reducing this burden, should be sent to the Chief Information Officer, U.S. Patent and Trademark Office, U.S. Department of Commerce, P.O. Box 1450, Alexandria, VA 22313-1450. DO NOT SEND FEES OR COMPLETED FORMS TO THIS ADDRESS. **SEND TO: Commissioner for Patents, P.O. Box 1450, Alexandria, VA 22313-1450.**

If you need assistance in completing the form, call 1-800-PTO-9199 and select option 2.

Figure 5G—Fee Transmittal Letter

PTO/AIA/15 (10-17)
Approved for use through 11/30/2017. OMB 0651-0032
U.S. Patent and Trademark Office; U.S. DEPARTMENT OF COMMERCE
Under the Paperwork Reduction Act of 1995 no persons are required to respond to a collection of information unless it displays a valid OMB control number.

UTILITY
PATENT APPLICATION
TRANSMITTAL

(Only for new nonprovisional applications under 37 CFR 1.53(b))

Attorney Docket No.	
First Named Inventor	
Title	
Priority Mail Express® *Label No.*	

APPLICATION ELEMENTS
See MPEP chapter 600 concerning utility patent application contents.

ADDRESS TO:
Commissioner for Patents
P.O. Box 1450
Alexandria, VA 22313-1450

ACCOMPANYING APPLICATION PAPERS

1. ☐ **Fee Transmittal Form**
   (PTO/SB/17 or equivalent)

2. ☐ **Applicant asserts small entity status.**
   See 37 CFR 1.27

3. ☐ **Applicant certifies micro entity status.** See 37 CFR 1.29.
   Applicant must attach form PTO/SB/15A or B or equivalent.

4. ☐ **Specification** [Total Pages _____]
   Both the claims and abstract must start on a new page.
   (See MPEP § 608.01(a) for information on the preferred arrangement)

5. ☐ **Drawing(s)** (35 U.S.C. 113) [Total Sheets _____]

6. **Inventor's Oath or Declaration** [Total Pages _____]
   (including substitute statements under 37 CFR 1.64 and assignments serving as an oath or declaration under 37 CFR 1.63(e))

   a. ☐ Newly executed (original or copy)

   b. ☐ A copy from a prior application (37 CFR 1.63(d))

7. ☐ **Application Data Sheet** * See note below.
   See 37 CFR 1.76 (PTO/AIA/14 or equivalent)

8. **CD-ROM or CD-R**
   in duplicate, large table, or Computer Program (*Appendix*)
   ☐ Landscape Table on CD

9. **Nucleotide and/or Amino Acid Sequence Submission**
   (if applicable, items a. – c. are required)

   a. ☐ Computer Readable Form (CRF)

   b. ☐ Specification Sequence Listing on:

      i. ☐ CD-ROM or CD-R (2 copies); or

      ii. ☐ Paper

   c. ☐ Statements verifying identity of above copies

10. ☐ **Assignment Papers**
    (cover sheet & document(s))
    Name of Assignee _____

11. ☐ **37 CFR 3.73(c) Statement**   ☐ **Power of Attorney**
    (when there is an assignee)

12. ☐ **English Translation Document**
    (if applicable)

13. ☐ **Information Disclosure Statement**
    (PTO/SB/08 or PTO-1449)
    ☐ Copies of citations attached

14. ☐ **Preliminary Amendment**

15. ☐ **Return Receipt Postcard**
    (MPEP § 503) (Should be specifically itemized)

16. ☐ **Certified Copy of Priority Document(s)**
    (if foreign priority is claimed)

17. ☐ **Nonpublication Request**
    Under 35 U.S.C. 122(b)(2)(B)(i). Applicant must attach form PTO/SB/35 or equivalent.

18. ☐ **Other:** _____
    _____
    _____
    _____
    _____

***Note:** (1) Benefit claims under 37 CFR 1.78 and foreign priority claims under 1.55 **must** be included in an Application Data Sheet (ADS).
(2) For applications filed under 35 U.S.C. 111, the application must contain an ADS specifying the applicant if the applicant is an assignee, person to whom the inventor is under an obligation to assign, or person who otherwise shows sufficient proprietary interest in the matter. See 37 CFR 1.46(b).

19. CORRESPONDENCE ADDRESS

☐ The address associated with Customer Number: _____ **OR** ☐ Correspondence address below

Name	
Address	

City		State		Zip Code	
Country		Telephone		Email	

Signature		Date	
Name (Print/Type)		Registration No. (Attorney/Agent)	

This collection of information is required by 37 CFR 1.53(b). The information is required to obtain or retain a benefit by the public which is to file (and by the USPTO to process) an application. Confidentiality is governed by 35 U.S.C. 122 and 37 CFR 1.11 and 1.14. This collection is estimated to take 12 minutes to complete, including gathering, preparing, and submitting the completed application form to the USPTO. Time will vary depending upon the individual case. Any comments on the amount of time you require to complete this form and/or suggestions for reducing this burden, should be sent to the Chief Information Officer, U.S. Patent and Trademark Office, U.S. Department of Commerce, P.O. Box 1450, Alexandria, VA 22313-1450. DO NOT SEND FEES OR COMPLETED FORMS TO THIS ADDRESS. **SEND TO: Commissioner for Patents, P.O. Box 1450, Alexandria, VA 22313-1450.**
If you need assistance in completing the form, call 1-800-PTO-9199 and select option 2.

Figure 5H—Patent Transmittal Letter

Patent Prosecution and the PTO

Acquiring a patent is a little like playing a board game. If you are the applicant, you must move the invention through the PTO examination process, avoiding certain obstacles—such as technical errors or delays—while preserving the strongest possible claims for patent protection. The process of shepherding a patent application through the PTO is known as "patent prosecution." In this chapter, we discuss the common elements of patent prosecution and provide background on PTO procedures.

RESOURCE

Examiners and applicants rely on three official resources during patent prosecution:

- **Patent statutes.** The patent laws passed by Congress are found in Title 35 of the United States Code (e.g., "35 U.S.C. §103" means Title 35 of the U.S. Code, Section 103).
- **Patent Rules of Practice.** The Patent Rules of Practice are administrative regulations located in Volume 37 of the Code of Federal Regulations (e.g., 37 CFR § 1).
- *Manual of Patent Examining Procedure* (**MPEP**). The MPEP is often referred to as the "examiner's bible" because it covers almost any situation encountered in patent prosecution. It contains the PTO's Rules of Practice and the patent statutes described below.

These resources can be obtained from the PTO's website, www.uspto.gov, and the CASSIS CD-ROMs at any PTDL. The PTO Rules of Practice and the patent statutes can also be found at regional government bookstores in paperbound form. Search online or in your local phone directory for the government bookstore nearest you.

CAUTION

Patent prosecution and foreign filing. Filing a U.S. patent application has an impact on the ability to obtain a patent in foreign countries. After an application is filed in the United States, an applicant may publish articles on the invention without loss of legal rights in the United States or in Convention countries (countries with which the United States has patent treaties) because the applicant will get the benefit of the U.S. filing date in all Convention countries. However, an applicant is not entitled to priority rights in the few remaining non-Convention countries, so the invention should not be published before actual filing in these countries. (For a list of Convention countries and information on international patent treaties and the relationship between U.S. and foreign filing, consult Chapter 9.)

Patent Prosecution: The Road to Allowance

Patent prosecution usually proceeds through the following steps:

1. The PTO's Office of Initial Patent Examination (OIPE) receives and catalogs the application, examines it for technical errors (such as an incorrect fee, informal drawings, missing pages in the application, and errors on the Application Data Sheet), and notifies the applicant of any mistakes, along with a time limit to make the necessary corrections—upon pain of abandonment if the corrections are not timely made.

2. If the applicant files electronically via the PTO's EFS-Web system (strongly recommended because there is a substantial additional charge and disadvantages for filing a paper application), the PTO provides a printable acknowledgment at the time of filing (which includes the serial number and date) and later sends an official filing receipt on paper. (If the application was filed in paper form, the PTO affixes a sticker with the application's serial number and filing date onto the self-addressed return postcard that applicants should send with the application and returns the postcard to the applicant.) In either case, a few weeks later it sends the applicant an official filing receipt (if the paper application is in order).

3. A PTO examiner examines and initially rejects (or sometimes "allows," that is, "accepts") the claims of the application.

4. The applicant responds to the rejection with an amendment.

5. The PTO examiner reviews the amendment and either issues a Notice of Allowance or makes a final rejection of the application.

The goal during patent prosecution is to obtain a Notice of Allowance, a statement from the PTO that the application meets the legal requirements of patentability and a statement that the issue fee is due. Of course, not all applications meet this standard. In the event the examiner sends a "final Office Action," there are still several options as discussed later in this chapter.

Receipt of Application

When the application is filed electronically, the PTO provides an instant, online acknowledgment at the time of filing, with the date of receipt or "deposit" date and an eight-digit number, for example, "U.S. Patent & TM Office, 22 August 2011; 11/801,666." The number is the serial number (sometimes called "application number") of the inventor's application. Maintain the serial number and filing date in confidence. If you enclose a return postcard with a paper application, the PTO will stamp and return this; it will be the first correspondence from the PTO (see Chapter 5). The postcard usually arrives within two to four weeks of filing, stamped with the same information found on the online acknowledgment. Within one to three months after you file an application on paper or electronically, the PTO mails you an official filing receipt. The filing receipt contains more detailed information, such as the name(s) of the inventor(s), the title of the patent application, the examining group to which the application has been assigned, the filing date and serial number of the application, and the number of claims (total and independent). This information is entered into the PTO's data-processing system. If the filing receipt has any errors, you should correct these by sending or faxing a brief letter to the Office of Initial Patent Examination (OIPE) of the PTO.

Once the official filing receipt is mailed, the patent application is officially pending. At this point, the invention and any descriptive literature can be labeled either as "Patent Pending" or "Patent Applied For" (both expressions mean the same thing; see "Patent Pending Status," below).

If the PTO's Office of Initial Patent Examination (OIPE) feels that you made an administrative error in the application, such as failing to sign a form or pay the fee, they will send a deficiency notice explaining what's required and sometimes also requiring a penalty fee. Once the applicant complies, the PTO will mail the filing receipt.

Patent Extensions: When the PTO Takes Too Long

As a result of a law passed in 1999 (35 U.S.C. § 154(b)), the term of a patent will be extended for as long as necessary to compensate for any of the following:

- any delay caused by the PTO failing to examine a new application within 14 months of filing
- any delay caused by the PTO failing to take any of the following actions within four months:
  - reply to an amendment or to an appeal brief
  - issue an allowance or Office Action after a decision on appeal, or
  - issue a patent after the issue fee is paid and any required drawings are filed.
- any delay caused by the PTO failing to issue a patent within three years of filing, unless the delay was due to the applicant filing a continuation or divisional application, or buying a delay to reply to an Office Action, or
- any delay due to secrecy orders, appeals, or interferences.

CAUTION

Filing the IDS. An Information Disclosure Statement (IDS; see Chapter 5) must be filed within three months of the application filing date or before the first Office Action.

Patent Pending Status

As explained in Chapter 1, an inventor has no patent rights until the patent actually issues. In other words, if an invention is "patent pending" and has not been published, it can be copied freely by anyone. The purpose of marking a device "patent pending" is to give notice to potential infringers. Most potential infringers won't copy a patent pending device because a patent may later issue and the money spent on expensive tooling would have been wasted. Although you cannot sue for patent infringement, it is possible to recover for infringements during the pendency period, provided that the application is published under the 18-month rule (see below), issues as a patent, and that the infringer had notice during the pendency period.

It's a criminal offense to use the words "patent applied for" or "patent pending" in any advertising when there's no active, applicable regular or provisional patent application on file.

TIP

Publication of pending applications. As a result of legislation passed in 1999, every pending application will be published for the public to view 18 months after its earliest effective filing date, or earlier if requested. However, if at the time of filing the applicant states that the application will not be filed abroad, the application will not be published. If the applicant later files the application abroad, the applicant must notify the PTO within 45 days that the application has been foreign filed and revoke the Non-Publication Request.

Any member of the public is allowed to cite prior art against any published application without the applicant's consent. The citation must be filed within two months of publication. An applicant whose application is published may obtain royalties from an infringer from the date of publication if the application later issues as a patent, provided the infringer had actual notice of the published application. The PTO charges a separate $300 fee for publishing an application and this fee will be due with the issue fee. (35 U.S.C. §§ 122, 154.)

First Office Action

Within six months to two years after the filing date, the applicant will receive correspondence from the PTO known as a "first Office Action" (sometimes called an "official letter" or "OA"). You can determine an approximate date when the PTO will send the first Office Action by looking in a recent *Official Gazette* under "Examining Corps." Look for the appropriate examining group. Also you can call the clerk of the examining group. The *Official Gazette* and PTO phone numbers are available on the PTO's website, www.uspto.gov.

The first Office Action may:

- cite and enclose copies of prior art that the examiner believes shows the applicant's invention is obvious or lacks novelty
- reject claims
- list defects in the specification or drawings, or
- raise other objections.

It is very rare that an application is allowed in the first Office Action. More often, the examiner rejects some or all of the claims. Some examiners make a "shotgun" or "shoot-from-the-hip" rejection, flatly rejecting all claims for questionable reasons. Examiners sometimes do this because of the time pressures of work at the PTO or sometimes to force the applicant to state more clearly the essence of the invention and its distinguishing features.

UNITED STATES DEPARTMENT OF COMMERCE
Patent and Trademark Office
Address : COMMISSIONER OF PATENTS AND TRADEMARKS
Washington. D C. 20231

SERIAL NUMBER	FILING DATE	FIRST NAMED APPLICANT	ATTORNEY DOCKET NO.
07/345,678	1998 Aug 9	LeRoy Inventor	

Portia Barrister
1237 Chancery Lane
Puyallup, WA 98371-3841

Received 1998 Oct 14 P. B.

EXAMINER	
HEYMAN, J	
ART UNIT	PAPER NUMBER
2540	3

DATE MAILED: 1998 Oct 9

This is a communication from the examiner in charge of your application.

COMMISSIONER OF PATENTS AND TRADEMARKS

Response Due 1999 Jan 9 P.B.

☑ This application has been examined ☐ Responsive to communication filed on _____ ☐ This action is made final.

A shortened statutory period for response to this action is set to expire __3__ month(s), __0__ days from the date of this letter.
Failure to respond within the period for response will cause the application to become abandoned. 35 U.S.C. 133

Part I THE FOLLOWING ATTACHMENT(S) ARE PART OF THIS ACTION:
1. ☑ Notice of References Cited by Examiner, PTO-892.   2. ☑ Notice re Patent Drawing, PTO-948.
3. ☐ Notice of Art Cited by Applicant, PTO-1449   4. ☑ Notice of Informal Patent Application, Form PTO-152
5. ☐ Information on How to Effect Drawing Changes, PTO-1474   6. ☐ _____

Part II SUMMARY OF ACTION

1. ☑ Claims __1-7__ are pending in the application.

Of the above, claims _____ are withdrawn from consideration.

2. ☐ Claims _____ have been cancelled.

3. ☐ Claims _____ are allowed.

4. ☑ Claims __1-7__ are rejected.

5. ☐ Claims _____ are objected to.

6. ☐ Claims _____ are subject to restriction or election requirement.

7. ☑ This application has been filed with informal drawings which are acceptable for examination purposes until such time as allowable subject matter is indicated.

8. ☐ Allowable subject matter having been indicated, formal drawings are required in response to this Office action.

9. ☐ The corrected or substitute drawings have been received on _____ . These drawings are ☐ acceptable; ☐ not acceptable (see explanation).

10. ☐ The ☐ proposed drawing correction and/or the ☐ proposed additional or substitute sheet(s) of drawings, filed on _____ . has (have) been ☐ approved by the examiner. ☐ disapproved by the examiner (see explanation).

11. ☐ The proposed drawing correction, filed _____ , has been ☐ approved. ☐ disapproved (see explanation). However, the Patent and Trademark Office no longer makes drawing changes. It is now applicant's responsibility to ensure that the drawings are corrected. Corrections MUST be effected in accordance with the instructions set forth on the attached letter "INFORMATION ON HOW TO EFFECT DRAWING CHANGES", PTO-1474.

12. ☐ Acknowledgment is made of the claim for priority under 35 U.S.C. 119. The certified copy has ☐ been received ☐ not been received ☐ been filed in parent application, serial no. _____ ; filed on _____ .

13. ☐ Since this application appears to be in condition for allowance except for formal matters, prosecution as to the merits is closed in accordance with the practice under Ex parte Quayle, 1935 C.D. 11; 453 O.G. 213.

14. ☐ Other

PTOL-326 (Rev. 7 - 82)   EXAMINER'S ACTION

Figure 6A—Sample Office Action

Serial No. 07/345,678

-2-

Art Unit 254

The drawing is objected to under Rule 1.83(a) in that all the features recited in the claims are not shown. See claims 1 and 2 regarding the "electronic counter means" and "first and second solid state counters."

The specification is objected to under Rule 1.71(b) as inadequate. In particular, there is insufficient information regarding the "counter," "counter memory," and how the counter controls the illumination of the lights. Applicant is required to amplify the disclosure in this regard without the introduction of new matter. 608.04 MPEP.

Claims 1-7 are rejected under 35 U.S.C. § 112, 1st paragraph, as based on an insufficient disclosure. See above.

Insofar as adequate, claims 1-6 are rejected under 35 U.S.C. § 102(b) as fully anticipated by Ohman. Ohman shows an electronic cribbage board counter that fully meets these claims. See Fig. 1. The microprocessor 300 shown in Fig. 3 inherently includes the counter means of claims 1 and 2.

Claim 7 is rejected under 35 U.S.C. § 112, ¶ 2. The term "said LCD readout" lacks proper antecedent basis in parent independent claim 1, as claim 1 recites only an "LCD monitor."

Figure 6A—Sample Office Action (continued)

Claim 7 is rejected under 35 U.S.C. § 103 as unpatentable over Ohman in view of Morin. Ohman shows an electronic cribbage board counter, as stated. Morin shows an LCD tally monitor. It would be obvious to substitute Morin's LCD tally monitor for Ohman's mechanical readout, because the substitution of LCD readouts for mechanical readouts is an expedient well known to those skilled in the art. See column 13, lines 34-41 of Morin, which indicate that in lieu of the LCD readout shown, other types of readouts may be used.

No claim is allowed.

The remaining art cited shows other electronic board games containing the claimed structure. Note Morin, which shows the details of a computer as containing first and second counter means.

Any inquiry concerning this communication should be directed to Examiner Heyman at telephone number 703-557-4777.

Heyman/EW

98/10/9

John S. Heyman

Examiner

Figure 6A—Sample Office Action (continued)

An example of an Office Action is provided in Fig. 6A. The first page of the OA details the examiner's objections to the application. The rule or law that is the basis for each objection is provided on Pages 2 and 3 of the OA. The objections include:

1. The drawing is not complete because it fails to show certain features that are recited in the claims. This objection is based on Patent Rule 1.83(a).

2. The specification is inadequate because it does not demonstrate in sufficient detail how to make and use the invention. This rejection is based on Patent Rule 1.71(b).

3. Because the specification is inadequate, the examiner rejects all claims because the claims are based on an inadequate specification. This objection is based on Section 112 of the patent laws. (35 U.S.C. § 112.)

4. Claims 1 to 6 are rejected because the examiner does not believe they are novel when compared to a prior patent (the "Ohman" patent). This rejection is based on Section 102 of the patent laws. (35 U.S.C. § 102.)

5. Claim 7 is rejected because there is no identical antecedent (or direct reference) in Claim 1. The applicant has failed to follow a technical drafting rule. This objection is based on Section 112 of the patent laws. (35 U.S.C. § 112.)

6. Claim 7 is rejected a second time as being obvious. The examiner believes that, based on two prior references (the Ohman patent and the Morin patent), this claim would have been obvious to someone skilled in the field of the invention.

This rejection is based on Section 103 of the patent laws. (35 U.S.C. § 103.)

If the examiner cites any prior-art references in the Office Action, those references will be listed on an attached page.

Amendment in Response to First Office Action

The first Office Action will specify the time period (usually three months) by which a response (known as an "amendment") must be filed. The response usually includes some or all of the following:

- amendments to the drawings, description, and/or claims
- a summary of the amendments
- a review of the rejections made by the examiner to the main claim
- a discussion of any technical (Section 112) rejections
- a review of the references cited by the examiner
- a statement of distinctions and arguments as to prior-art references
- a request for reconsideration of the examiner's position
- a discussion of dependent and other main claims
- a request that the claims all be allowed and that examiner write the claims, and
- a conclusion.

The Applicant's Duty to Disclose

If you are the applicant, you have a duty to disclose all information known to you, such as relevant prior art, which bears on the patentability of the invention (see Chapter 2). If a prior-art reference is found that is so similar that it makes your invention unpatentable, your application should be abandoned. Other than this, as general rule, you do not have to (and shouldn't) admit or state anything negative about your invention.

Most rejections of claims are based upon prior art and are categorized either as Section 102 rejections (the invention is not novel) or Section 103 rejections (the invention is novel but obvious). If the rejection is based on Section 103, and there is no Section 102 rejection, the examiner is tacitly admitting that the claims are novel.

If a prior-art reference is strikingly similar to the claim, the claim is said to "read on" the prior art. In these cases, the claim must usually be amended, usually by narrowing it.

Formerly, if an inventor could prove that the date of invention was earlier than the effective date of the reference, the applicant could "swear behind" and eliminate the reference. However under the America Invents Act, applicants are no longer allowed to swear behind any reference; the filing date of the application (or any earlier provisional patent application from which priority is claimed in the later-filed regular patent application) is the earliest date that a patent applicant can rely upon.

If an applicant wants to authorize email communications, the following statement must be included in the application: *"Recognizing that Internet communications are not secure, I hereby authorize the PTO to communicate with me concerning any subject matter of this application by electronic mail. I understand that a copy of these communications will be made of record in the application file."*

Nothing New May Be Added

An applicant can never add new matter to an application (Section 132 of the patent statutes). New matter is any technical information, including dimensions, materials, and so on, that was not present in the application as originally filed.

TIP
Web filing and fax available. Anyone can file a new application via the Internet using the PTO's EFS-Web system. This saves the need to make a file copy, use Express Mail, prepare a receipt postcard, a check for the filing fee, wait several weeks to get the postcard back, and pay a surcharge (presently $200

for a small entity and a micro entity) for filing a paper application. In addition, subsequent papers and fees (amendments, petitions, appeals, and elections) can be filed via the Internet if the applicant is a registered eFiler. Although an application cannot be faxed, subsequent papers can be filed by fax. Faxed papers must include a statement, *"I certify I have transmitted this paper by fax to the Patent and Trademark Office at* [time] *on* [date]." The PTO will consider the paper as having been filed on the date of transmission, or the next business day if the applicant faxes it on a nonbusiness day.

The PTO has provided email addresses and Internet access for many of its employees. Email communications may be used for minor matters, such as status requests, minor corrections in a paper, notification that a communication has been sent, and more, but not major papers, such as amendments and patent applications. The email address for PTO employees is usually provided on office actions. Because email is not a secure form of communication and the PTO is obligated to preserve all patent applications in secret, PTO employees are not allowed to send email containing any sensitive information unless specifically authorized by the applicant.

Second and Final Office Action

A second Office Action, usually designated a "final" Office Action, is mailed within two to six months of filing the first amendment. This is supposed to end the prosecution stage, but a "final action" is rarely final.

When the Second Office Action Isn't Final

In some cases, the examiner's second Office Action may not be final—for example, if the examiner cites new references that were not necessitated by the applicant's amendments. In that case, the applicant responds as if it were a first Office Action.

Notice of Allowance, Issue Fee, and Official Patent Deed

If the amendment is sufficient and the examiner is convinced that the application meets the requirements of patentability, they will send a Notice of Allowance which will state that prosecution is closed and an issue fee is due within three months. A "Notice of Allowability" is sometimes mailed with or before the Notice of Allowance. This document merely states that the claims are all allowed and a Notice of Allowance is attached (or will be sent soon) and indicating whether formal drawings are due.

Several months after the fee is paid and formal drawings are filed (if necessary), an Issue Notification is sent from the PTO indicating the issue date and number of the patent. On the Tuesday that the patent issues, the PTO mails the official "Letters Patent" deed.

Challenges after issue. Under the America Invents Act (AIA), a new post-grant review (PGR) procedure allows anyone to challenge a patent on any invalidity ground for nine months after the patent issues. However the standard and the fees are high: The challenge must initially show that it is likely that at least one claim of the patent is unpatentable, or a novel and unsettled legal question is involved. If you're aware of another's patent that you feel should not have issued, and your evidence meets the criteria, and you are willing to forgo the right to use the evidence in court, file for a post-grant review within nine months after issuance. The fee for requesting PGR is an astronomical: $20,000, plus a fee of $27,500 for instituting the proceeding. (37 CFR § 42.15(a)(1)&(2).)

Reviving the Dead: Recovering From Technical Abandonment

An Office Action requiring substantive changes usually requires that a reply be made within three months from the mailing date of the Office Action. An Office Action requiring nonsubstantive changes usually requires a reply within one month. The period for reply will be included on the cover page of every Office Action. If these deadlines are not met, the application is technically abandoned, meaning that it cannot be pursued further at the PTO. However, the application can usually be "revived" or extended in any of the three following ways:

- **Buying an extension (PTO Rules 136(a) and 17(a)–(d)).** If a reply is not made within the designated period, it can still be made at any time up to the sixth month from the Office Action mailing date by buying an extension from the PTO. The extension cannot be purchased to extend any response period beyond six months and also can't extend the three-month statutory period from the Notice of Allowance.

- **Petition to revive if delay was "unavoidable" (PTO Rules 137(a) or 316(b), and 17(c)).** A petition can be filed to revive the application within six months of the date of abandonment if the delay was "unavoidable," for example, if the Office Action was never received or the applicant suffered a severe illness.

- **Petition to revive if delay was avoidable but unintentional (PTO Rules 137(b) or 316(c), and 17(m)).** A petition can be filed to revive the application within the three-month period if the delay was "avoidable but unintentional," for example, if the applicant misinterpreted the time to reply to the Office Action. The fee for an "Avoidable-but-Unintentional" delay is usually much higher than that for an "Unavoidable" delay.

Responding to a Final Office Action

A "final" Action doesn't mean that PTO prosecution has ended; it means that the examiner is cutting off the applicant's right to change the claims in the application for the present filing. The applicant has the following options.

Convincing the Examiner

An applicant can ask the examiner to reconsider a final Office Action. This can be done in writing, by phone, or in person. Another amendment, known as an "after-final amendment," can also be filed. If the examiner is not convinced, an "advisory action" will be sent reiterating the examiner's position. The applicant still has the opportunity to exercise the other choices in this section.

Complying If the Examiner Suggests Changes

Sometimes an examiner will issue a final action containing a suggestion for amending the claims in a way that will place them in condition for allowance. If you are willing to make the suggested amendments—that is, they don't narrow the scope of your coverage too much—you should amend them as suggested; the examiner will then allow the application.

Complying With the Examiner's Request

The claims can be amended as suggested by the examiner; if the applicant does this as prescribed, the examiner will allow the application.

Buying the Right to Have a Submission Considered After Final Action

Under a new procedure, which is in a trial period, an applicant can change the claims after a final action and have them considered by the examiner by paying a fee. (Rules 129 and 17(r).) As of this writing, the fees are $220/$440/$880 for micro, small, and large entities, respectively.

Filing a Continuation, Continuation-in-Part, or a Request for Continued Examination

An inventor can have claims reviewed further by the examiner by filing a continuation application or a request for continued examination (RCE).

The continuation application is a new application you can file while the original (or "parent") application is still pending. A continuation application consists of the same invention, cross-referenced to the parent application and with a new set of claims.

An RCE is a cheaper way to file a continuation since you don't have to file a whole new application: You just file an RCE Request with the RCE fee and an amendment containing a new set of claims. You don't have to file a new copy of the specification or drawing, and you will not receive a new serial number or filing date.

The continuation and RCE both allow a second or third bite at the apple because it's theoretically possible to file an unlimited sequence of continuation applications. In both cases, the filing date of the parent application is retained for purposes of determining the relevancy of prior art.

> EXAMPLE: Jim filed a patent application for his paint roller invention in January 2017. He filed a continuation application for the paint roller in July 2019. Bob invented the same paint roller device in January 2018. Jim has priority because his first (parent) application was filed before Bob invented his paint roller.

A less common form of extension application is known as a continuation-in-part (CIP) in which a portion or all of the earlier application is continued and new matter not disclosed in the earlier application is included. CIP applications are used when an applicant wants to present an improvement but is prevented from adding it to a pending application because of the prohibition against adding "new matter" (see "Nothing New May Be Added," above).

EXAMPLE: Luther invents a bicycle gear with a new shape. After Luther files the patent application, his research shows that the gear works much more quietly if it's made of a certain alloy. Luther wants to add a few dependent claims specifically to cover a gear made of the alloy. The solution: File a CIP describing the alloy in the specification and add a few dependent claims that recite that the gear is made of the alloy. To avoid any possibility of double patenting, Luther abandons the parent application or files a terminal disclaimer, a statement that both patents will terminate on the date when the first patent ends.

An inventor who files a CIP usually allows the parent application to go abandoned because if the claims in the CIP and parent application are similar, one or both of the resulting patents can be held invalid under a principle known as double patenting. If the claims are different, both applications can proceed. (For further information on continuations, review MPEP § 201.07.)

TIP

Continuations and the 20-year term. If a continuation, CIP, or divisional application is filed, the resulting patent will expire 20 years from the filing date of the original, or parent, application.

Appeal

An applicant who believes that the examiner's final Office Action is wrong can appeal to the Patent Trial and Appeal Board (PTAB), a tribunal of PTO judges. In addition to filing written arguments, an oral hearing can be requested during which oral statements can be provided for 20 minutes. For further information on complying with the appeal procedure, see PTO Rules of Practice 191 to 198. The fees for appealing are expensive: $420 to file the Notice of Appeal and $1,050 to "forward" the brief to the Appeal Board.

> ## Petitions to the Commissioner for Nonsubstantive Matters
>
> In cases where unfair or illegal treatment is alleged, the Commissioner of Patents and Trademarks has the power to overrule almost anyone in the PTO except the PTAB. For example, if someone in the PTO's application branch decides that an application is not entitled to a certain filing date, the applicant can petition the Commissioner to overrule this decision. If the final Office Action is premised on unfair or illegal treatment, a petition that includes a verified statement signed by the applicant must be filed promptly. Verified statements are either notarized or contain a declaration attesting to the truthfulness of the statement.

After the appeal brief is filed, the examiner reexamines the application and files a response, usually maintaining the rejection (the "Examiner's Answer"). An applicant can file a response to the Examiner's Answer. The Board either agrees with the applicant and instructs the examiner to allow the application or the appeal is rejected (which happens in two-thirds of appeals) and the final office action stands. The applicant can file a further appeal to the Court of Appeals for the Federal Circuit (CAFC) within 60 days of the decision. If the CAFC upholds the PTO's decision, the applicant can request that the United States Supreme Court hear the case, although the Supreme Court rarely hears patent appeals. If a patent is finally issued as a result of an appeal, the PTO will extend the patent term up to five years based on the delay. (35 U.S.C. § 154.)

Abandonment

If a response to the final Office Action is not filed within the three-month period, the PTO mails a Notice of Abandonment and the application process is officially over.

> (i) **TIP**
> **Keeping others from pursuing your abandoned application.**
> The PTO had a Statutory Invention Registration (SIR) program under which an applicant who decided to abandon an application but also wanted to prevent anyone else from getting a valid patent on the same invention, could convert the application to a SIR. This would preclude anyone else from obtaining a patent on the invention with the exception of someone who filed before the applicant. However the AIA terminated the SIR Program in 2011. As a practical matter, an inventor can obtain the same result at a lesser cost by publishing the invention on the Internet or by having an invention registration company, such as ITD, Technotec, or *Research Disclosure* magazine, publish it.

Additional Application Issues

In this section, we discuss interferences, divisional applications, reissue applications, substitute applications, and double patenting. All of these topics relate to problems that may arise during patent prosecution.

Interferences Are Gone

The America Invents Act (AIA) terminated interference proceedings as of March 16, 2013. (An interference was a costly, complex PTO proceeding between two or more patent applicants or patentees to determine who invented the subject invention first.) The AIA has partially replaced interferences with a process known as derivation proceedings. A patent owner can bring a derivation hearing at the USPTO against another patent owner claiming to have the same invention and who has an earlier effective filing date. A derivation proceeding may be filed if the applicant in the later-filed application believes and can prove that an applicant with an earlier filing date copied or illegally derived the invention from the former. The derivation hearing request must be filed within a one-year period beginning on the date of the first publication of a claim in the earlier filed application.

Alternatively, the owner of a patent may sue the owner of another patent that claims the same invention and has an earlier effective filing date. These lawsuits can only be brought if the invention claiming priority was derived directly from the person seeking relief.

Divisional Applications

If a patent application contains more than one invention, the PTO will require that it be "restricted" to just one of the inventions. That's because the application fee entitles an applicant to have only one invention examined. Generally speaking, it's very difficult to successfully argue against (or "traverse") this type of PTO-imposed restriction. The solution to protect additional inventions claimed in the original application is to file a divisional application on them. The official definition of a divisional application is "a later application for a distinct or independent invention, carved out of a pending application and disclosing and claiming only subject matter disclosed in the earlier or parent application" (MPEP § 201.06). A divisional application is entitled to the filing date of the parent case for purposes of overcoming prior art. The divisional application must be filed while the parent application is pending.

CAUTION

When the public protests against allowance. If a member of the public, such as another inventor, is aware of information that is adverse to a pending application, this information may be brought to the attention of the examiner in the form of a protest by sending the information to the PTO and identifying the application as specifically as possible.

NASA Declarations

If an application relates to aerospace, the PTO will send the applicant a form letter (PTOL-224) with the filing receipt or after the application is allowed. The letter will state that because the invention relates to aerospace, a declaration is required stating the "full facts" regarding the making of the applicant's invention. This is to guarantee that NASA has no rights in it. A Notice of Allowance will not be issued if the declaration isn't filed.

Reissue Applications

A reissue application is an attempt to correct information in an issued patent. It is usually filed when a patent owner believes one of the following:

- The claims are not broad enough.
- The claims are too broad (the applicant discovered a new reference).
- There are significant errors in the specification.

In these cases, an attempt is made to correct the patent by filing an application to have the original patent reissued at any time during its term. The reissue patent will take the place of the original patent and expire at the same time as the original patent would have expired. If an applicant wishes to broaden the claims of the patent through a reissue application, the applicant must do so within two years from the date the original patent issued. An applicant may not use a reissue application to "recapture" subject matter that was previously given up during the prosecution process—for example, if an application purposely limited claims during prosecution, the applicant may not use the reissue process to broaden the claims back to their former state. In addition, a reissued patent may not be used to sue an infringer whose product did not infringe the claims of the patent as granted but does infringe the broader claims of the reissued patent. This is known as the "doctrine of intervening rights"—that is, the right to continue with a product would otherwise infringe an issued patent. There is a risk in filing a reissue application because all of the claims of the original patent will be reexamined and can be rejected.

Substitute Applications

If a patent application is abandoned, a substitute application can be filed that is essentially a duplicate of the abandoned application. (See MPEP § 201.09.) The disadvantage of a substitute application is that the filing date of the previously abandoned patent application is not retained. Any prior art occurring after the filing date of the earlier case can be used against the substitute case. If the substitute application issues into a patent, the patent will expire 20 years from the filing date of the substitute.

Double Patenting

If a patent is issued and the patent owner files a second application containing the same invention ("double patenting"), the second application will be rejected, or if the second application resulted in a patent, that patent will be invalidated. What does it mean when two applications contain the same invention? It means either that the two inventions are literally the same or that the second invention is an obvious modification of the first invention.

> EXAMPLE: An inventor applied for a patent on polymer dispersants used in motor oil to keep engines clean. A patent issued in 1989. A continuation application was filed incorporating similar, but slightly broader claims. The Court of Appeals for the Federal Circuit ruled that the continuation application was invalid for double patenting because it was an obvious modification of the first application. (*In re Emert*, 124 F.3d 1458 (CAFC 1997).)

In the example above, the applicant could avoid double patenting by agreeing that both patents would terminate on the date when the first patent ended (known as a "terminal disclaimer"). However, an applicant cannot file a terminal disclaimer to avoid double patenting if both inventions are the same.

Design Patent Prosecution

Design patent prosecution is much simpler than regular patent prosecution and rarely requires more than elementary changes. Usually, the examiner tells the applicant exactly what to do.

The drawings are the key element because the claims in a design patent are presented visually, not by words. To be patentable, the appearance of the applicant's design, as a whole, must be nonobvious to a designer of ordinary skill over the references (usually earlier design patents) cited by the examiner. Because many companies may modify their patented designs, multiple design patent applications are often filed to separately claim the various ways that the design may be embodied.

Unless the applicant pays for expedited processing, under the expensive "rocket docket" procedure (the petition fee was $1,600/$800/$400 (large/small/micro entity) as of January 2021), acquiring a design patent usually takes a few months to a year from date of filing. Design patents automatically expire 14 years after they're issued and cannot be renewed. There are no maintenance fees. An applicant can convert a design application to a utility application, or vice versa, by filing a continuing application under 35 U.S.C. Section 120. However, this is rarely done as it is very difficult to convert a design application to a utility application without adding new matter (see "Nothing New May Be Added," above).

Patent Ownership

The patent owner is the person entitled to control the manufacture and sale of the invention. For some patents, this can mean the beginning of a business dynasty that lasts long after the patent expires. For example, if Clarence Birdseye had not owned a patent for packaging frozen foods, or John Mason had not owned the patent for Mason jars, it is unlikely their respective companies would be here today. This chapter is about the issues that arise when inventors, employers, or coinventors assert ownership rights. First, we discuss the single inventor's situation. Next, we discuss the situation where an inventor gives up complete or partial ownership to an employer, usually under an employment agreement. Finally, we address the complications of joint patent ownership—for example, when more than one person creates a patentable invention.

The Inventor Is Initial Owner of Patent Rights

An inventor is an "idea" person who creates or discovers the inventive concepts that make the invention different and nonobvious and become the basis for the patent claims. (The claims are the "heart" of the patent application and are described in Chapter 5.) Unless the inventor has assigned the patent rights to someone else, or is employed to invent (discussed below), the inventor is the default patent owner, and can exploit the patent in two ways: by licensing or selling (assigning) rights to others; or by creating a company that manufactures and sells the invention.

For many inventors, licensing and assigning a patent are preferable to starting a manufacturing business. A license is permission for others to make use of or sell the invention for a limited period of time in exchange for royalty payments. An assignment can be a complete or partial transfer of patent ownership. Assignments are almost always made in return for payment, although in rare cases, an inventor may assign patent rights in order to benefit humanity. For example, Dr. Frederick Banting had no interest in the money from his pioneering process of controlling diabetes through insulin injections, so he assigned his patent rights to the University of Toronto. The primary difference between assignments and licenses is that the patent owner retains ownership during the license, but gives up patent ownership for an assignment.

Employee Inventions

Generally, most employed inventors are obligated to transfer rights in their inventions to their employer. This occurs in one of three ways:

- An employment agreement includes provisions that require the employee to give up all rights in advance of creating an invention. Because these employment agreements are signed before the employee creates the invention, they are sometimes referred to as preinvention assignments.
- The employee was hired specifically for the purposes of creating an invention (a principle known as "employed to invent," or "hired to invent").
- The employer acquires limited patent rights under a principle known as a "shop right."

RESOURCE

The subject of employee inventions is covered in more detail in *Profit From Your Idea: How to Make Smart Licensing Deals,* by Richard Stim (Nolo).

Employment Agreements

The majority of businesses that employ inventors, designers, and engineers require each employee to sign an employment agreement that establishes the circumstances under which the business owns employee-created inventions.

For example, in 1974, a scientist for the Minnesota Mining and Manufacturing Company (3M) was singing in a church choir when he realized that an adhesive substance produced at 3M could be affixed to paper and used to mark sections in his hymnal without damaging the book.

The result was Post-It notes, one of the most successful office products in history. Although the scientist conceived of the idea on his own time, he had signed an employment agreement with 3M that contained a preinvention assignment provision covering all inventions made by the employee that related to 3M's business. That's how 3M acquired (some might say "retained") all rights in the invention of Post-It notes.

Most preinvention assignments require that the employee-inventor assign all inventions to the employers that are:

- made during the term of employment
- related to the employer's existing or contemplated business
- made by using the employer's time (that is, the time for which the employee is paid), facilities, or materials, or
- made as a result of activity within the scope of the employee's duties.

If the employee disregards the agreement and attempts to patent and license an invention, the employer will be able to sue for breach of the employment agreement, and if the employer wins the lawsuit, the employee may have to pay monetary damages and transfer ownership of the patent to the employer.

Under many employment agreements, even if an employee makes an invention at home, on the employee's own time, the employer can still be entitled to ownership. Equally important, the employed inventor is usually bound to disclose all inventions to the employer (so the employer can determine if they're assignable).

Disclosing an invention simply means that the employee-inventor must report the invention; it does not necessarily mean that the inventor must give up rights. The final determination depends on the terms of the employment agreement and the law of the state in which the employee inventor works (see "Limitations on Preinvention Assignments," below).

If, after disclosure, the employer isn't interested in the invention, the employee can apply for a release. This is a document under which the employer reassigns or returns the invention to the employee. The employer may retain a "shop right" under the release. A shop right is a nontransferable right to use the invention for its own purposes and business only.

Who Is Listed in the Patent Application

Under the prior patent law, the inventor had to always be named as the applicant in a patent application even if the inventor had made a preinvention assignment. However, after September 16, 2011, an assignee of the invention may file the application on behalf of the inventor and without the inventor's signature.

Previously, if an employer filed a patent application for an invention made by an employee, the employee was the applicant and signed an assignment (a legal transfer) of the invention and the patent application to the employer at the time the employee signed the patent application. (If the employee refused to sign the assignment, the employer could sue the employee to compel the employee to sign the assignment; the employer can sue at any time, even after the patent issues.)

Under current law, if an employee has agreed to assign all inventions made in the course of employment to the company, the employer can file the patent application in its name or the employee's name. However, the employee must file an oath with the application and must also file an assignment of the application before the application issues.

Assignments are filed with the PTO. An assignment gives the employer all rights in the patent. The employer may be listed in the patent as the applicant or the assignee (owner), depending on how the application is filed. In any case, the employee will be listed as the inventor.

Some companies give the employee a cash bonus when the employee signs a company patent application. This bonus is not payment for signing (the employee's wages are supposed to cover that) but to encourage employees to invent and turn in invention disclosures on their inventions. Some employers give their inventor-employees a cut of the royalties from their inventions. Some will even set up a subsidiary entity (partly owned by the employee-inventor) to exploit the invention. Most, however, prefer to reward highly creative employees via the salary route.

Under current patent law, employers may want to consider revising employment agreements and assignments to indicate that each signing inventor authorizes the filing of the assigned application and that each signer is the original inventor (or joint inventor of a claimed invention). Including this language in an assignment will satisfy the current legal requirements.

Employment agreements also usually require the employee to keep good records of inventions made, to cooperate in signing patent applications, and to give testimony when needed, even after termination of employment. In addition, these agreements often contain a "power of attorney" provision that guarantees the employer can register and administer the ownership rights without the employee, even if the employee is willing and able to assist.

Employed to Invent

It is possible that even without a written employment agreement, an employer may own rights to an employee-created invention under the "employed to invent" doctrine. How does this rule apply? If an inventor is employed—even without a written employment agreement—to accomplish a defined task, or is hired or directed to create an invention, the employer will own all rights to the subsequent invention. This doctrine is derived from a Supreme Court ruling that stated, "One employed to make an invention, who succeeds, during his term of service, in accomplishing that task, is bound to assign to his employer any patent obtained." (*Standard Parts Co. v. Peck*, 264 U.S. 52 (1924).)

Generally, most companies prefer to use a written agreement because it is more reliable and easier to enforce than this implied agreement. However, the issue of "employed to invent" still arises. For example in one case, an engineer had no written employment agreement with his employer and was assigned as the chief engineer on a project to devise a process of welding a "leading edge" for turbine engines. Even though there was no preinvention assignment, a court held that the company owned the patent rights because the engineer was hired for the express purpose of creating the process.

Limitations on Preinvention Assignments

To protect employees, eight states impose restrictions on the permissible scope of assignments of employee-created inventions. These restrictions apply only to "inventions" an employee creates—that is, items for which a patent is sought. The California restrictions are typical. Under California law, an employee cannot be required to assign any of his or her rights in an invention he or she develops "entirely on his or her own time without using the employer's equipment, supplies, facilities, or trade secret information" unless:

- When the invention was conceived or "reduced to practice" (actually created or a patent application filed) it related to the employer's business or actual or "demonstrably anticipated" research or development.
- The invention resulted from any work performed by the employee for the employer. (Cal. Lab. Code § 2870.)

These limitations on employee invention assignments are not very generous to employees. The only inventions an employee can't be required to assign to the employer are true independent inventions—those that are developed completely without company resources and that don't relate to the employee's work or the employer's current business or anticipated future business.

The following states impose restrictions similar to California's:

- Delaware (Del. Code Ann. tit. 19, § 805.)
- Illinois (765 Ill. Comp. Stat. § 1060/2.)
- Kansas (Kan. Stat. Ann. § 44-130.)
- Minnesota (Minn. Stat. Ann. § 181.78.)
- North Carolina (N.C. Gen. Stat. §§ 66-57.1, 66-57.2.)
- Utah (Utah Code Ann. §§ 34-39-2, 34-39-3.), and
- Washington (Wash. Rev. Code Ann. §§ 49.44.140, 49.44.150.)

Under several states' laws (including California, Illinois, Kansas, Minnesota, and Washington), an employer must provide you with written notice of your state's restrictions on an employer's right to obtain an assignment of employee inventions. If this is not done, the assignment could be unenforceable. What if you live in one of the states that do not have laws restricting invention assignments? Even in most of these states, preinvention assignments can't be grossly unfair to employees.

Shop Rights

The previous two situations (written employment agreements and the "employed to invent" rule) allow the employer to become the owner of all patent rights. There is another situation in which the employer may not acquire ownership of the patent or trade secret, but may acquire a limited right, known as a "Shop right," to use these innovations. Under a shop right, the employee retains ownership of the patent, but the employer has a right to use the invention without paying the inventor.

A shop right can occur only if the inventor uses the employer's resources (materials, supplies, or time) to create an invention. Other circumstances may be relevant, but use of employer resources is the most important criterion. Shop-right principles are derived from state laws and precedents in court cases. Generally, the shop-right claim arises when an inventor sues a former employer for patent infringement. The employer defends itself by claiming a shop right.

For example, in 1982, a consultant for a power company was hired to install and maintain an electrostatic precipitator. However, the power company was not happy with the operation of the device. The consultant, observing the problems, conceived of an innovation that would detect particles of ash. The power company installed the device at several locations and the consultant, who later filed for and acquired a patent, sued for infringement. A federal court ruled that the power company had a shop right because the consultant had developed the invention while working at the power company and using the power company's resources. This shop-right situation is distinguished from the "employed to invent" scenario because in the shop-right case, the consultant's invention was not the subject of the consulting contract—he was not hired to invent. However, because he used the power company's resources to create the invention, the company acquired a shop-right.

An inventor should be concerned about shop rights only if the invention is created on the employer's time or using the employer's resources (materials, supplies, or trade secrets). If it isn't, the shop-right rule does not apply.

University Employee Inventions

Most colleges and universities require that faculty execute formal agreements that grant the university rights to all discoveries made by employees using its labs, equipment, or other resources. Normally, when an invention or discovery is successful and results in a licensing deal, the school pays some portion of the revenues to the inventor. At one major university, for example, inventors get 50% of the first $100,000 of net revenue, 40% of the second $100,000, and 30% of any sums after that. But if there's no ownership agreement, the deal might be quite different, as demonstrated in the example below.

> **EXAMPLE:** In the mid-1960s, Robert Cade, a professor of medicine at the University of Florida, created a high-energy drink that provided electrolyte replacement for perspiring athletes. The potion eventually came to be sold under the trademark Gatorade. At the time, the University of Florida and Dr. Cade had no written agreement regarding the ownership of employee-created inventions. On his own, Cade licensed Gatorade to a food company and started reaping huge revenues. The university felt it should own the rights to the drink and sued. Also, the government got into the suit because it provided grants for Cade's research. After a long three-party lawsuit, the parties settled and the university was reportedly awarded 20% of the professor's share. The university's share is estimated to be over $4 million a year from the licensing of the Gatorade formula. The Gatorade drink generates over $1 billion in annual sales.

TIP

Inventions prepared under government contracts. According to a federal policy implemented in 1983, federal agencies may waive or omit patent rights when awarding government contracts (although there are some exceptions for space research, nuclear energy, and defense). If an inventor contracts directly with the federal government—and is not working for the federal government through a private company—the inventor should ask about patent ownership at the time of contracting.

Joint Owners

When more than one person creates a patentable invention, the joint inventors share credit in the patent application and share in the patent ownership as joint patent owners. However, to acquire joint-inventor status, each person must contribute an inventive concept that becomes part of at least one patent claim. Unfortunately, issues about joint ownership often lead to contentious disputes between inventors. For example, the diabetes researcher, Dr. Banting, was so angered by an associate taking credit for his insulin research, that he tackled him at the university, knocking his head against the floor. As indicated in the following sections, most joint-owner disputes are less violent and more concerned with the issue of compensation. The primary issue is often whether an associate is entitled to coinventor status.

Establishing and Proving Joint Inventorship

As proving coinventor status can sometimes be difficult, the best way to avoid problems is for all inventors to keep a lab notebook. A lab notebook is a technical diary which faithfully records all developments and is frequently signed by the inventor(s) and witnesses. In Chapter 3, we discuss record keeping and inventor notebooks. In addition, many disputes can be avoided by the use of a consultant's agreement in which persons working with an inventor agree to assign all rights in their work to the inventor. Absent such documentation, or agreement, expensive disputes can arise, with only vague memories to deal with.

Joint inventors need not have worked together either physically or at the same time, and each need not have made the same type or amount of contribution. To qualify as a joint inventor, as stated, an inventor need merely have contributed something to at least one claim of the application.

Determining whether a contribution is substantial can sometimes be difficult. For instance, if one person came up with the concept of the invention, while the other merely built and tested it—the second person is not a coinventor. It is not enough to build and test an invention. The joint inventor must make a contribution to at least one novel and nonobvious concept that makes the invention patentable.

On the other hand, if one person came up with the idea for an invention and the model maker then came up with valuable suggestions and contributions that went beyond the skill of an ordinary model maker and made the invention work far better, both people should be named as coinventors on the patent application, provided the model maker's contribution is present in at least one claim.

> **EXAMPLE:** Dr. Wilcox developed a device that could be attached to a computer modem and could triple its output. However, Dr. Wilcox was stumped as to how to increase the input. Sarah, an engineering student constructing his device, suggested a novel compression method that allowed Dr. Wilcox to triple the input telephone transfer rate. Sarah's contribution found its way into the claims of a patent application. Dr. Wilcox and Sarah are joint inventors.

When a Patent Application Fails to List Joint Inventors

If an error is made in listing the inventors on a patent application, and the mistake was made with deceptive intent, it can affect the ability to enforce the patent and may result in loss of patent rights. For example, if a biotech company, in bad faith, fails to name two additional inventors in its chromatography patent, a court can prevent the company from enforcing patent rights against a competitor.

If the error in the patent was not made in bad faith, the mistake can be corrected without any loss of rights under PTO Rule 48 (patent applications) or PTO Rule 324 (patents). (See Chapter 6 for more information on correcting patents.)

Patent Laws and the Effect of Joint Ownership

Usually, the joint owners decide amongst themselves how to split the revenue from sales and licensing under the terms of a joint-owner agreement. If the joint owners cannot decide and a dispute results, a court will make the final determination. However, there are some special rules regarding joint ownership and division of income from patents. All joint owners must consent to an assignment of all rights to the patent. In other words, no joint owner can give up *all* rights in an invention since the joint owner does not own the whole invention. However, unless prohibited by an agreement with the other owners, any joint owner can make, sell, or use the invention without the consent of the other owners and without compensating the other owners. This is the result of a patent law that states, "In the absence of any agreement to the contrary, each of the joint owners of a patent may make, use, offer to sell, or sell the patented invention within the United States, or import the patented invention into the United States, without the consent of and without accounting to the other owners." (35 U.S.C. § 262.)

This statute may prevent a joint owner from being rewarded for any inventive contribution. In the case of an investor who has purchased a patent interest, the statute can prevent the investor from being rewarded for making a capital contribution. The statute also creates a severe hardship if one joint owner works hard to engineer and develop a market for the patented product and another joint owner steps in as a competitor. Seem unfair? The only way for the joint owners of a patented invention to protect their interest is to enter into a Joint Ownership Agreement, as provided below.

Joint Ownership Agreements

Problems commonly arise in situations where there are joint owners. These include questions as to who is entitled to commercially exploit the invention, who owns the financial shares, and what type of accounting must be performed on partnership books. In addition, the inequitable results of Section 262 of Title 35 of the U.S. Code may deprive a patent owner of reward for invention or investment. Fortunately, most of these problems can be minimized or eliminated by the use of a joint-ownership agreement (JOA).

A typical JOA:

- prohibits any joint owner from exploiting the patent without the other joint owners' consent, except that if there is a dissenter, a majority can act if consultation is unsuccessful
- provides a method of resolving disputes, for example, in case of an equally divided vote, the parties will select an arbiter, whose decision shall break the tie
- provides that the joint owners shall share profits proportionately, according to their interests in expenditures and income. In the event that one owner does not agree to an expenditure, the others can advance the amount in question, subject to an increased reimbursement (often double the expenditure) from any income, and
- provides that if an owner desires to manufacture or sell the patented invention, that owner must pay a reasonable royalty to all other owners, including the manufacturing owner.

RESOURCE

Copies of joint ownership agreements can be found in *Patent It Yourself,* by David Pressman and Thomas Tuytschaevers (Nolo) and in *Profit From Your Idea: How to Make Smart Licensing Deals,* by Richard Stim (Nolo).

Methods of Acquiring Joint Ownership

In the previous sections, we described how joint invention leads to joint ownership. However, there are methods of acquiring a joint-ownership interest other than by invention. Below we highlight some examples.

Joint ownership created by assignment for money. In return for a payment or for other investment in the invention process, an inventor may convey a portion of a patent to an investor.

EXAMPLE: Tom invents a metal detector that works underwater. He needs money to build a prototype and to promote the invention. Jerry agrees to give Tom $100,000 in return for an assignment of 50% ownership interest in the invention. Tom and Jerry become joint owners. However, Jerry would not be listed in the patent application as an inventor, only as the assignee of a partial interest in the invention.

Joint ownership created by will. Upon the death of a patent owner, the patent rights, like any property right, can be passed to two or more heirs or beneficiaries.

EXAMPLE: Sam patents a process for scrambling and cooking eggs within their shells. He dies and in his will he leaves half ownership interest in the invention to his daughter Carol, and the other half to Dartmouth College. Carol and Dartmouth become joint owners.

Joint ownership created by assignment to a partnership. If a patent owner transfers a patent to a partnership, each partner becomes a joint patent owner.

EXAMPLE: Jill invents a new style of camping stove. Ian wants to invest money to perfect the invention. Jim, a lawyer, wants to contribute his legal and licensing experience to help license the invention. Jill, Ian, and Jim form a partnership and Jill assigns the invention to the partnership. Each partner is a joint owner in the invention. ●

Patent Infringement

Patent infringement is the unauthorized making, using, selling, offering for sale, or importing of a patented invention. Allowing patent infringement to occur can have disastrous results for a patent owner, as revenues and market share from a patented invention are siphoned away by a competitor. On the other hand, the results may be even more disastrous if the owner sues the competitor and the patent is successfully challenged. For example, Hoffman-LaRoche, an international drug company, sued a smaller company, Promega, over the use of a patent for a process for analyzing DNA. Promega successfully defended itself by arguing that the DNA patent was invalid because the inventors had misled patent examiners. The ruling allows anyone to use, sell, or make the patented invention freely even though Hoffman-La Roche paid $300 million for the patent. As you can see, enforcing patent rights can be expensive, and sometimes risky. In this chapter, we discuss the different ways that a patent can be infringed and the different procedures for dealing with infringement.

What Is Patent Infringement?

Infringement occurs when someone makes, uses, sells, offers for sale, or imports a patented invention without permission from the patent owner (or, also without permission, files an application with the FDA to approve a new drug that is the subject of a patent). These types of acts are referred to as "direct infringement."

- To **make** an infringing invention means to construct or manufacture the parts of the patented device without permission from the owner. For example, a patent on an electronic key ring is infringed when a factory manufactures the key rings without permission.
- To **use** an infringing invention means to practice (or use) an invention without the permission from the patent owner. For example, a patent on a process for making an integrated circuit chip is infringed every time the process is used to make a chip.

- To **sell** an infringing invention means to sell a patented invention without permission from the patent owner.
- To make an **offer to sell** an infringing invention can include solicitations and advertisements—for example, if a company emails a proposal to sell an infringing device.
- To **import** an infringing invention means to bring a patented invention into the United States without permission from the patent owner. For example, a company infringes when it imports a patented automobile spark plug into the United States without the U.S. patent owner's authorization.

It can also be an infringement to contribute to or persuade someone else to do one of the acts described above. We discuss these acts of indirect infringement later in this chapter.

Defendants and Plaintiffs

The terms "plaintiff" and "defendant" are used throughout this chapter. The plaintiff is usually the patent owner who believes that a patent has been infringed and initiates a lawsuit. The defendant is the party accused of infringement.

Only Patent Claims Can Be Infringed

To infringe a patent, the infringing device must physically have or perform all of the elements contained in at least one of the patent claims. (See Chapter 5 to learn more about patent claims.) A device containing additional elements will also infringe. For example, if a patent claim recites three elements, A, B, and C, and the infringing device has four elements, A, B, C, and D, it will infringe. But if the infringing device has only two of the three elements, A and B, it won't infringe. If this concept, which uses the principle "more is less," is a little strange to you, a good analogy is a computer search system, where the more terms you use for your search, the fewer hits you will get and vice versa. Also, if the allegedly infringing device has the three elements, A, B, and C, but one of the elements is materially different from the element recited in the patent, then there is no infringement. (A dependent claim is read as if the entire claim it refers to is incorporated into the dependent claim. Thus a dependent claim that reads "2. A telephone as in claim 1 wherein said handset has a particle microphone" does not claim just the particle microphone, but as if the entire phone as described in claim 1 were included as part of claim 2.)

Patent Owner's Permission

An essential element of infringement is that it occurs without the patent owner's authorization. When a patent owner has authorized a use, anything that exceeds that authorization is also an infringement. For example, a company that was authorized to build and use one machine built two machines, although it only used one at a time. The building of the second machine was an infringement.

When a Patent Can Be Infringed

A patent can be infringed only "during the term of the patent." This means that the patent must be issued and maintenance fees must be paid up in order for the patent owner to sue for infringement. A patent owner cannot sue for infringement during the "pendency period," that is, the time between filing of the patent application and issuance of the patent.

However, under the new 18-month publication statute, an inventor whose application is published prior to issuance may obtain royalties from an infringer from the date the application is published. There are two requirements: (1) The application later issues as a patent, and (2) The infringer had actual notice of the published application. (35 U.S.C. §§ 122, 154.) (Again, infringement must be limited to what is claimed in the patent.) An infringer will have actual notice of a publication if he or she sees the published application. This can be accomplished by sending a copy to the infringer by certified mail.

Direct and Indirect Infringement

When a patent owner sues for infringement, a court must examine the patent claims, the defendant's device or process, and the defendant's actions to determine if infringement has occurred. A device or process can infringe a patent if it duplicates all of the elements in at least one patent claim ("direct infringement"). Indirect infringement can occur when someone contributes to or persuades another to infringe.

Direct Infringement

A defendant may commit direct infringement by either directly making, using, importing, selling, or offering for sale a device or process that meets every element of a patent claim of the patented invention (called literal infringement) or by designing around the patent claims to achieve the same function in substantially the same manner and with the same result. This is known as "equivalent infringement," or infringement under the "doctrine of equivalents."

In a literal infringement, the defendant's device is literally the *same* invention as that described in the patent claim. For example, a company devised an improved pH meter to measure acidity. In an attempt to recapture market share, a competitor committed literal infringement by copying the patented meter and mounting system and each element of the company's claim was met by the copier's device. (*Rosemount, Inc. v. Beckman Instruments, Inc.*, 727 F.2d 1540 (Fed. Cir. 1984).)

A patent claim can specifically describe (or "recite") the function of one of the items instead of describing its structure. This type of clause is known as a means-plus-function clause (also known as a "means for" clause) because it usually starts with the word "means."

For example, a patent claim recites "a means for storing textual information" and does not specifically state any type of storage device. In a literal infringement of a "means for" clause, a court must conduct an inquiry to determine if a storage device used in the defendant's invention is the same as or equivalent to that described in the patent's specification to support the means-plus-function clause. For example, a means for storing information could be described in the specification as a CD-ROM. If there's a means-plus-function clause, not all devices that meet the means plus function will infringe; only those described in the specification (or equivalents). (35 U.S.C. § 112.) Not every use of "means" will trigger this analysis. If the clause is specific enough, and the infringing device meets the "means" clause, the means-plus-function equivalency is unnecessary. (*Cole v. Kimberly-Clark Corp.*, 102 F.3d 524 (Fed. Cir. 1996).)

Even if a device is not a literal copy of a patented invention, it can be an infringement if it performs substantially the same function in substantially the same way and obtains the same result as the patented invention. This doctrine of equivalents was created to prevent infringers from "designing around" the patent claims by making minor alterations or by using later developments that weren't available when the patent application was filed.

In 2000, a federal appeals court ruled that a patent owner could not assert any element of a patent claim in an infringement lawsuit if that element was amended (including voluntary amendments) during the patent prosecution process. In other words, the appeals court ruling barred the use of the doctrine of equivalents for any amended patent claim. In 2002, the U.S. Supreme Court struck down this absolute bar to the doctrine of equivalents and replaced it with a less arbitrary standard. Under the Supreme Court's standard, all amended claims are presumed to be narrowed so as to bar the doctrine of equivalents. But this presumption can be rebutted if a patent owner can demonstrate that the amendment involved a feature that was "unforeseeable at the time of the application" or "for some other reason" could not be included in the original claim. In summary, patent owners who amended their claims prior to or after the Supreme Court's decision can still use the doctrine of equivalents if they can overcome the presumption that the amendment surrendered the equivalents at issue. (*Festo Corp. v. Shoketsu Kinzoku Kabushiki Co. Ltd.*, 535 U.S. 722 (2002).)

Indirect Infringement: Contributory; Inducing

Indirect infringement can occur in two ways: when someone is persuaded to make, use, or sell a patented invention without authorization "inducing infringement"; see 35 U.S.C. § 271(b), or when a material component of a patented invention is sold with knowledge that the component is designed for an unauthorized use. ("Contributory infringement"; see 35 U.S.C. § 271(c).)

Contributory Infringement

Contributory infringement cannot occur unless there is a direct infringement. It is not enough to sell parts necessary for creating a patented invention; those parts must be used in an infringing invention.

> EXAMPLE: A company owned a patent for a device that removed sulfur from flue gas. A manufacturer sold parts to assemble the patented device without authorization. However, the manufacturer was not liable for contributory infringement because it took more than five years to construct the devices and they would not be completed until after the patent expired. (*Joy Techs. v. Flakt*, 6 F.3d 770 (Fed. Cir. 1993).)

Contributory infringement requires an awareness by the seller that the parts being sold will be used to assemble an infringing invention.

> EXAMPLE: A company patented an apparatus and method for connecting sections of metal ducts used in heating and air conditioning systems. A manufacturer was a contributory infringer because it knowingly sold the specially shaped corner pieces (that had no use other than in the patented duct-connecting system) to purchasers of the patented machines. (*Met-Coil Systems Corp. v. Korners Unlimited, Inc.*, 803 F.2d 684 (Fed. Cir. 1986).)

Inducing Infringement

Inducing infringement does not require actual knowledge of infringement.

EXAMPLE: A company, SEB, patented a "cool touch" deep fryer whose exterior was cool to the touch. GlobalTech Appliances, operating outside the United States, copied everything but the cosmetic aspects of the SEB deep fryer. GlobalTech then branded these deep fryers for sale by Sunbeam, Montgomery Ward, and others. SEB sued GlobalTech for inducing others to infringe its cool-touch patent. GlobalTech defended itself by arguing that it couldn't induce others to infringe because it had no actual knowledge it was infringing SEB's patent. (GlobalTech had vetted its device with a patent attorney but had failed to disclose to the attorney that their device was copied directly from the SEB deep fryer.) The Supreme Court ruled for the patent owner, SEB. The Court said that inducing infringement required knowledge of the existing patent, but that knowledge could be inferred using a legal standard referred to as "willful blindness." As the Court stated: "Many criminal statutes require proof that a defendant acted knowingly or willfully, and courts applying the doctrine of willful blindness hold that defendants cannot escape the reach of these statutes by deliberately shielding themselves from clear evidence of critical facts that are strongly suggested by the circumstances." The Court went on to distinguish willful blindness from a lower court's standard known as "deliberate indifference." As for the differences, the bottom line is that when asking an attorney to render a legal opinion ("Does my deep fryer infringe?"), don't hide information (like, "I copied this from another deep fryer"). (*GlobalTech Appliances v. SEB*, 563 U.S. 754 (2011).)

Inducement of infringement requires direct infringement. In a 2014 case, the Supreme Court unanimously ruled that there is no liability for induced patent infringement—encouraging someone else to infringe—unless there has been direct (or actual) patent infringement. In that case, Akamai exclusively licensed a patent for delivering data. Limelight was accused of inducing infringement. However Limelight never directly infringed the patent because it did not carry out all of the steps claimed in the method. Instead, Limelight's customers carried out one of the steps. Because there was no direct infringement, the Supreme Court concluded there could be no inducement to infringe. (*Limelight Networks, Inc. v. Akamai Technologies, Inc.*, 572 U.S. 915 (2014).)

Out of This World Infringement

Patent law states that a U.S. patent can be infringed in outer space if it is made, used, or sold in outer space on a "space object" under the jurisdiction or control of the United States.

Design Patent Infringement

The scope of rights of a design patent depends upon its drawings, not its claims (which merely repeat the title of the design patent).

In 2008, the Court of Appeals for the Federal Circuit ruled, in *Egyptian Goddess, Inc. v. Swisa, Inc.*, that design patent infringement should be determined by a single test, as follows: A design patent is infringed if an ordinary observer would think that the accused design is substantially the same as the patented design when the two designs are compared in the context of the prior art.

A defendant accused of infringing a design patent may attempt to prove that the design patent is invalid. One common defense is to argue that the design lacks ornamentality based on the fact that the design is of no concern to consumers.

Since a design patent covers only the device's ornamental nonfunctional features, it is not an infringement to copy nonpatented functional features that are associated with the design patent. For example, if a musician obtains a patent on a uniquely shaped guitar knob, it is not an infringement to copy functional, nonpatented elements of the knob, such as the screw-mechanism by which the knob is affixed to the guitar. When an infringed design patent is a component of an "article of manufacture," the award of damages is limited to revenues attributable to the component (not to the complete article).

Activity Within U.S. Borders

A U.S. patent owner cannot stop the manufacture, use, or sale of inventions in a foreign country unless the owner has patented the invention in that country (see Chapter 9). However, it is an infringement:

- to import an infringing device into the United States
- to create all of the parts of a patented invention and ship those parts to a foreign company with instructions for assembly, and
- to import or sell, offer to sell, or use in the United States a product made by a process patented in the United States.

Inadvertent Infringement

For purposes of determining infringement, it doesn't matter whether a party independently develops an identical invention or inadvertently copies an invention. Any unauthorized sale, use, or manufacture qualifies as an infringement, regardless of the intent or knowledge of the defendant.

Intent and knowledge do matter for two related issues: damages and contributory infringement. The amount of money awarded to a patent owner for infringement ("damages") may vary depending on the infringer's intent. A "willful infringer," that is, someone who knew of the plaintiff's patent and deliberately infringed, may have to pay more. In order to be liable for contributory infringement, a company must know that the item supplied is being used to create an infringement.

Who Can Sue, Who Can Be Sued?

The patent owner can sue any manufacturer who makes, uses, sells, imports, or offers for sale any device or practices any process covered by the claims of a patent. The patent owner can sue the retailer or ultimate purchaser of the invention (including a private individual) as well as the manufacturer.

Under a theory known as vicarious liability, a business such as a corporation or partnership is liable for infringements committed by employees or agents when any of the following is true:

- The agent acts under the authority or direction of the business.
- The employee acts within the scope of employment.
- The business benefits, adopts, or approves the infringing activity.

A company that purchases another company may be liable for infringements committed by the purchased company under a standard known as successor liability. Successor liability occurs in any of the following cases:

- There is an agreement between the companies to assume liability.
- The two companies merge.
- The purchaser is a "continuation" of the purchased business.
- The sale is fraudulent and made to escape liability.

Because the location of the lawsuit depends on the location of the defendant, lawsuits against the retailer or customer are sometimes brought in order to find a court that's geographically close to the patent owner. If a suit is brought against a retailer or customer, the manufacturer of the infringing device usually must step in and defend or reimburse the customer's suit. If the infringer is an out-of-state manufacturer and the local retailer is sued, it places a burden on the manufacturer to defend at a distance.

> ⊘ **CAUTION**
>
> **When governments infringe.** The U.S. government (or contractors making products under a government contract) can be liable for infringement if a patented invention is used or manufactured by or for the United States without authorization. However, the only remedy is financial damages and interest. (The only forum where the United States can be sued is the U.S. Court of Claims in Washington, D.C.) The patent owner cannot obtain a court order halting the government infringement. In a 1999 decision, the Supreme Court ruled that under the Constitutional principle of sovereign immunity, states are not liable for patent infringement, even though Congress passed a law making them liable. (*Florida Prepaid Postsecondary Ed. Expense Bd. v. College Savings Bank*, 527 U.S. 627 (1999).)

Stopping Patent Infringement

Patent laws are like stop signs along the road; people are supposed to obey them, but some do not. Often the only way to enforce patent laws is to drag the infringer into a federal court and obtain a court order prohibiting infringement and requiring the infringer to pay damages. In the following sections, we discuss the elements of patent litigation and the remedies available under patent law. We discuss alternatives to patent litigation later in this chapter.

Patent Litigation

We have highlighted some common elements of patent litigation below.

The "Cease and Desist" or "Offer of License" Letter

The cease and desist letter is the first volley in an infringement lawsuit and accomplishes the following as it:

- informs the alleged infringer of the patent, that is, provides evidence of the patent's validity and ownership
- requests that infringing activity be stopped. This may or may not include a threat of litigation (see "When the Defendant Fires the First Shot: Declaratory Relief," below), and

- requests that damages or a royalty for past infringement be paid to the patent owner.

When the Defendant Fires the First Shot: Declaratory Relief

If a company reasonably believes that it will be sued for infringement— for example, because it received a cease and desist letter—it can sue the patent owner in a federal court for declaratory relief. This asks the court to determine the validity of the patent and whether it has been infringed. In recent years the right to seek declaratory relief has been broadened by court decisions, so that even if an infringer receives an "offer to license" letter, it may have the right to sue for declaratory judgment (DJ). Most experts warn that almost any patent notification letter will not entitle the infringer to sue for a DJ, but some say that it is still safe to send a letter merely notifying the infringer of the existence of the patent and inviting the infringer to consider and discuss it.

Jurisdiction and Venue

Federal district courts have the exclusive right to determine patent infringement disputes (known as "exclusive jurisdiction"). The patent owner must determine which federal court is the proper geographic location (venue) for the litigation. A lawsuit for patent infringement may be brought in the district where the defendant's residence is located, or where the defendant has committed acts of infringement and has a regular and established place of business. If the defendant is a corporation, the Supreme Court has held that patent owners can sue corporate defendants only in districts where the defendant: (1) is incorporated, or (2) has committed acts of infringement *and* has a regular and established place of business. (*TC Heartland LLC v. Kraft Foods LLC*, 137 S. Ct. 1514 (2017).) Lawsuits for patent infringement against the U.S. government must be filed in the Court of Claims in Washington, D.C.

Complaint and Summons

The plaintiff in a patent infringement lawsuit initially prepares three documents: a complaint, a summons, and a civil cover sheet. These three documents must be filed with the federal court and delivered to the defendant under the federal court's rules of service of process.

The complaint for patent infringement sets forth the facts of the infringement and requests remedies such as compensation and injunctive relief for the infringement. If the plaintiff desires a jury trial, that demand should be made in the complaint. If the plaintiff has not sought a jury trial but the defendant wants one, the request for a jury trial should be made in the defendant's answer.

The Answer

The "answer" is a response to the complaint in which the defendant admits or denies the statements and provides a list of defenses.

Counterclaims

If the defendant wishes to bring an action against the plaintiff based on an issue related to the plaintiff's complaint, a counterclaim must be filed at the time the answer is filed. A counterclaim is compulsory, meaning it must be brought if it arises out of the same transaction or occurrence that is the subject of the complaint. For example, a patent owner, angry over illegal copies, assaults the president of the company making the infringements. If the patent owner sues the president for infringement, the president must assert his claim for damages for the assault in his counterclaim.

Discovery

"Discovery" is a process by which each party to the litigation acquires information for trial. The discovery may include requests for documents or may be in the form of written questions (interrogatories or requests for admissions). A party or witness may also be deposed (interviewed under oath) before a court reporter. Discovery, especially a deposition, is extremely expensive and its cost often induces parties to settle lawsuits.

Protective Orders

Patent litigation often requires investigation and discovery of information that is confidential. The parties may agree to protect and limit the disclosure of such information. The court may also issue a protective order prohibiting public disclosure of the information.

Expert Witnesses

Often, the technical and scientific nature of patent law demands that experts in the field testify on behalf of each party. Before trial, each party identifies its expert witnesses by means of a document known as "Identification of Expert Witness."

In 2004, the Court of Appeals for the Federal Circuit indicated that a patent owner of a complex technology will have a difficult time proving infringement unless expert witness testimony is provided. (*Centricut LLC v. Esab Group, Inc.*, 390 F.3d 1361 (Fed. Cir. 2004).)

Trial

The process of trying a case in front of a judge or jury is beyond the scope of this book. However, we can summarize some of the events that occur. The trial begins with opening statements from the parties followed by presentation of the plaintiff's case and then the defendant's case. Because of the large number of technical terms and scientific language, the parties often use visual aids and expert witnesses as explanatory devices. For example, the parties may simplify the procedure by creating a glossary of terms or using enlarged copies of claims or charts comparing the claims to the invention. Some attorneys use charts to illustrate the sequence of events from conception of the invention to the issuance of patents.

Each side attempts to prove the elements of its case. For example, if one side is asserting a defense, all the elements necessary to prove that defense are introduced through witnesses or through physical evidence such as documents. The witnesses for each side are cross-examined, that is, questioned by the attorneys for the opposing counsel. After each side has presented its case, the two sides summarize their positions in a final statement.

A patent case can be heard in front of a judge, or if either party elects, it can be heard in front of a jury with a judge presiding. There are some issues that a jury is not permitted to decide. For example, under a recent Supreme Court ruling, a jury may not interpret the patent claims. An interpretation may be made only by the judge. This is usually accomplished before trial in a proceeding known as a *Markman* hearing. A jury may determine whether infringement has occurred and the amount of damages.

After the jury deliberates and issues a verdict, the verdict is confirmed by the judge and becomes a judgment that can be enforced by the prevailing (or winning) party. A judgment is the relief (or denial of relief) awarded by the court as the result of the judge or jury's verdict. If the judgment is in favor of the patentee, it will usually award the patentee monetary damages and an injunction (a court order prohibiting the defendant from infringing any more). On some occasions, the judge will set aside the jury's verdict because the judge may feel that the verdict is not supported by the law and facts.

Appeal

If either party is unhappy with the decision of the federal court, the case can be appealed to the United States Court of Appeals for the Federal Circuit (known as "CAFC" or the "Federal Circuit") in Washington, D.C., and which occasionally travels around the country to hear appeals. The Federal Circuit was established in order to bring about uniformity in the application of the patent laws.

A three-member panel of judges will review the trial court record to determine if a legal error occurred. If the parties are not satisfied with the Court of Appeals' determination, the only other recourse is to the U.S. Supreme Court. However, the U.S. Supreme Court rarely hears patent cases, so the CAFC's determination is usually final.

Remedies

A patent owner has several legal remedies for infringement. The owner can:

- obtain a court order preventing the infringing activity
- halt importation of infringing devices
- recover compensatory damages, and
- in exceptional cases, recover triple damages and attorneys' fees.

Injunction

A court can stop all infringing activity through a written order called an injunction. The injunction can be granted at the end of a trial (a permanent injunction) or the patent owner can attempt to halt the infringing activity immediately, rather than wait for a trial. The patent owner may seek a court order halting the activity for a short period of time (known as a temporary restraining order or TRO). The TRO only lasts a few days or weeks. A temporary restraining order may be granted without notice to the infringer if it appears that immediate damage will result, for example, that evidence will be destroyed.

The TRO remains in effect until the court has an opportunity to schedule a hearing for the preliminary injunction where both parties have an opportunity to present evidence. The preliminary injunction lasts until the final judgment has been rendered. Two factors are used when a court determines whether to grant a preliminary injunction. First, is the plaintiff likely to succeed in the lawsuit? Second, will the plaintiff suffer irreparable harm if the injunction is not granted? For example, the maker of a plastic cervical extrication collar was entitled to a preliminary injunction against the manufacturer of a competing plastic collar. A judge determined that the patent owner had a likelihood of success and the patent owner would suffer serious damage if sales of the infringing device were allowed to continue. (*California Med. Prods. v. Emergency Med. Prods.*, 796 F.Supp. 640 (D. R.I. 1992).)

In a 2006 case involving the auction site eBay, the Supreme Court determined that courts should not automatically issue an injunction based on a finding of patent infringement. (Alternatively, an injunction should not be denied simply on the basis that the plaintiff does not make, sell, or use the patented invention.) Instead, a federal court must still weigh the four factors traditionally used to determine if an injunction should be granted. The case is seen as a blow to patent trolls—patent holders that do not make or sell products but who sue others who use the patented technology. (*eBay v. MercExchange, L.L.C.*, 547 U.S. 388 (2006).)

When a TRO or preliminary injunction is issued, the court requires that the party seeking the injunction post security money or a bond. The security is intended to cover the costs and damages in case the defendant prevails.

Halting Importation of Infringing Devices

If an infringing device is being imported into the United States, the patent owner can sue the importer, distributor, retailer, or end user or alternatively may bring a proceeding before the International Trade Commission. An ITC trial proceeds rapidly and usually is over within a year after suit is filed. If the patent owner wins, the ITC will issue an exclusion order, which it sends to the president. If the president approves the exclusion order, Customs will block the infringing products at the port of entry.

Compensatory Damages

A patent owner can recover money from the defendant as compensation for the damage from the infringement. These damages can include any profits lost as a result of the infringement. When determining lost profits as damages in a patent infringement case, two questions are

asked: (1) How many of the infringer's historical sales would not have
been made absent the infringing feature or invention? and (2) How
many of those sales would have been made by the patent owner if the
infringer had not been competing in the marketplace? In 2003, the
Court of Appeals for the Federal Circuit established that as for the
first question, when a patent owner seeks damages for more than one
patent, the patent owner must distinguish the effects of each patent on
marketability. For example, what is the effect if one of several infringing
patents were invalid? As for the second question, the court determined
that an effective analysis of the marketplace competition requires going
beyond broad categories of products and providing evidence of actual
competitive patterns as to the accused products. (*Ferguson Beauregard/
Logic Controls v. Mega Sys.*, 350 F.3d 1327 (Fed. Cir. 2003); *Utah Medical
Products v. Graphic Controls Corp.*, 350 F.3d 1376 (Fed. Cir. 2003).) The
Supreme Court has ruled also that in certain situations—where a party
supplies components that infringe a patent under Section 271(f)(2) of Title
35 of the U.S. Code—the patent owner can recover for lost foreign profits.
(*WesternGeco v. ION*, 138 S. Ct. 2129 (2018).)

A patent owner can also recover damages for infringement as a
royalty based on what the patent owner would have obtained from the
sale of the defendant's device. For example, a court might examine what
royalties the patent owner would have received if it had licensed the
defendant's sale of the infringing device. The owner of a utility patent is
not entitled to the defendant's profits resulting from infringement. However, the owner of a design patent can recover the defendant's profits.

As a requirement for recovering damages, any patent owner who
sells the patented product must mark the patented device with the patent
number. If the owner fails to mark the device, damages can be recovered
only from the date that the patent owner notifies the infringer. Even if
the patented invention is unmarked, a court can still order a halt to the
sale or manufacture of the infringing device.

Apportioning Damages in Design Patent Infringement

In a 2017 case, Apple claimed that a Samsung phone model infringed design features of the Apple iPhone and its interface. A jury found for Apple and the court awarded (with interest) $399 million dollars, based on all of Samsung's profits from the phone model. The Supreme Court held that damages should not be awarded from the entire profits of Samsung phone sales but only the profits attributable to that aspect of the smartphone's appearance that were infringed. (*Samsung Electronics Co. v. Apple Inc.*, 137 S. Ct. 429 (2017).)

Increased Damages and Attorneys' Fees

In exceptional cases, financial damages may be increased, at the discretion of the court, up to triple the award (known as "enhanced damages"). In addition, a court may also award attorneys' fees to the winning side. An exceptional case would be one in which infringement is willful (the defendant knew of the plaintiff's patent and deliberately infringed). The CAFC has held that treble damages are generally reserved for "egregious cases of culpable behavior."

For example, a company patented a method of masking sounds and licensed the patent rights to a company. The license was later terminated but the former licensee continued to make and sell the device. On that basis, the damages were tripled and the defendant was required to pay the patent owner's attorneys' fees. (*Acoustical Design, Inc. v. Control Elecs. Co.*, 932 F.2d 939 (Fed. Cir. 1991).)

In 2016, the Supreme Court instructed judges to exercise their discretion when considering enhanced damages. Courts were instructed to put more emphasis on the state of mind of the infringer, and less on the objective reasonableness of the infringer's possible defenses. (*Halo Electronics, Inc. v. Pulse Electronics, Inc.*, 136 S. Ct. 356 (2016).)

Failure to Obtain "Green Light" Letter Does Not Imply Willfulness

It's common for a company preparing to sell a new invention to get an opinion from a lawyer indicating whether the invention infringes existing patents (known as a "green light" letter). If a company accused of infringement did not obtain a green light letter, a court would then infer that the reason for failing to get the opinion was that the company believed or knew that its invention infringed. A court faced with this situation would conclude that the infringement was willful and order more severe penalties. The Court of Appeals for the Federal Circuit reversed this 20-year precedent when it ruled that the absence of an opinion of counsel is only one of several factors to be considered when determining if patent infringement is willful. (*Knorr-Bremse Systeme fuer Nutzfahrzeuge GmbH v. Dana Corp. et al.*, 383 F.3d 1337 (Fed. Cir. 2004).)

Defenses to Patent Infringement

A defendant in a patent infringement lawsuit usually argues that the patent owner's patent is invalid. Alternatively, it can argue that even if the patent is valid, the defendant's product or process does not infringe. Other defenses include arguing that the infringement is excused or that the patent owner has misused the patent or has unclean hands. Below, we examine some common patent defenses.

Lack of Standing

A plaintiff who doesn't own patent rights lacks the legal capacity (or "standing") to bring the lawsuit. For example, a company sues a former employee for copying a patented software program. The employee proves that he, not the software company, owns the patent. Therefore, the software company lacks standing and the case will be dismissed.

Patent Invalidity

A lawsuit for patent infringement almost always becomes two separate battles: one in which the plaintiff claims damage from infringement, and the other, in which the defendant attempts to terminate the patent rights by proving the patent is invalid. For example, in one case, the Polaroid company sued Kodak for infringement of ten patents related to instant photography. The court determined that Kodak infringed seven Polaroid patents, but that the other three of Polaroid's patents were invalid.

To prove that a patent is invalid, the defendant commonly attacks the patent on the basis of lack of novelty or nonobviousness. In general, all of the criteria used by the PTO to grant a patent are reexamined by the defendant at trial. The defendant will usually attempt to show prior art that anticipates or renders the patent's claims obvious or try to prove that sales or disclosure of the patented invention occurred more than one year prior to filing the patent application.

For example, a company was sued for infringement of a patented device for displaying computer text on a television monitor. The defendant proved that the company had submitted a proposal for sale of the invention more than one year prior to filing its patent application. On that basis, the patent was invalidated and there was no infringement. (*RCA Corporation v. Data General Corporation*, 887 F.2d 1056 (Fed. Cir. 1989).)

Another basis for invalidity is where the patent is indefinite. In 2014, the Supreme Court held that a patent could be invalid for indefiniteness if its claims failed to define the scope of the invention with "reasonable certainty." This is a more relaxed standard than the previous "insolubly ambiguous" standard. The Court's decision may make patent claims easier to invalidate, a boon to those fighting off patent trolls but a bane for those trying to pursue infringers. (*Nautilus, Inc. v. Biosig Instruments, Inc.*, 134 572 U.S. 898 (2014).)

Proving invalidity requires clear and convincing evidence. In a 2010 case, the Supreme Court refused to alter the standard for invalidating a patent in a battle between two tech companies. Microsoft was sued for patent infringement by i4i, a Canadian company, over an XML feature of Microsoft's *Word* software. At trial, Microsoft argued that i4i failed to disclose a prior invention that might have invalidated the application (a principle known as the "one-year rule"). The jury was instructed that the patent could only be invalidated if there was "clear and convincing" evidence of invalidity. Microsoft and many other tech companies wanted the court to use the lower standard of "preponderance of the evidence" which would make it easier to invalidate many of the iffy patents owned by nonpracticing entities (also known as patent trolls). The Justices refused to change the standard, although the Court made one concession to troll victims: They could tell juries about any evidence that hadn't been considered by the Patent Office, such as facts Microsoft had advanced about i4i's patent. (*Microsoft Corp. v. i4i Limited Partnership*, 131 564 U.S. 91 (2010).)

In 2015, the Supreme Court ruled that a good-faith belief of invalidity is not a defense to inducement. In that case, Commil owned a patent for implementing short-range wireless networks. Cisco did not infringe the patent, but its customers did when they utilized a combination of Cisco devices and software. Commil sued Cisco for inducing infringement. At trial, Cisco was prevented from defending itself by claiming it had a good-faith belief that Commil's patent was invalid. The Supreme Court agreed with the trial court and refused to establish a defense "of belief in invalidity." The high court also ruled that, in order to bring a claim of patent inducement, the patent owner must show proof that "the defendant knew the acts were infringing." (*Commil v. Cisco*, 575 U.S. 632 (2015).)

Inequitable Conduct

A defendant may attempt to prove that a patent owner intentionally misled a patent examiner or should have known that withheld information was material (important) to the examination process. In that case, the issued patent is invalid. This defense is known as "inequitable conduct."

Exhaustion (First Sale Doctrine)

Once a patented item is sold, rights to that item are exhausted and it is not an infringement to resell it. This defense is commonly known as either the "first-sale exemption" or the "exhaustion doctrine." This defense does not apply if someone purchases an infringing invention, one that was initially sold without authorization from the patent owner. For example, this defense is not available if a company purchases infringing sparkplugs and resells them at retail outlets.

In 2008, the Supreme Court ruled that a customer who purchases a patented product from an authorized licensee cannot be sued for infringement. In other words, the patent owner's rights are exhausted after the first sale of the patented product. (*Quanta v. LG Electronics*, 553 U.S. 617 (2008).)

Repair Doctrine

It is not an infringement to repair a patented device and replace worn-out unpatented components. It is also not contributory infringement to sell materials used to repair or replace a patented invention. This defense does not apply for completely rebuilt inventions or for unauthorized inventions, items that are made or sold without authorization from the patent owner.

For example, a company owned a patent for a convertible top apparatus used in automobiles. The fabric used in the top was not patented. Under the repair doctrine, the sale of fabric to legitimate purchasers of the patented convertible top was not an infringement or contributory infringement. However, a second company was making an infringing version of the convertible top apparatus. Any repair on these devices was an infringement. The sale of fabric for these infringing devices was a contributory infringement. *(Aro Mfg. Co. v. Convertible Top Replacement Co.*, 365 U.S. 336 (1961).)

File Wrapper Estoppel

The official file of a patent application is stored at the Patent and Trademark Office and is known as a "file wrapper." All statements, admissions, correspondence, or documentation relating to the invention are placed in the file wrapper. If, during the patent application process, the inventor admits limitations to the invention or disclaims certain rights, those admissions or disclaimers will become part of the file wrapper and the patent owner cannot later sue for infringement over any rights that were disclaimed in the file wrapper. This defense is known as file wrapper estoppel (or prosecution history estoppel). Estoppel means that a party is prevented from contradicting a former statement or action.

For example, a medical company owned a patent for an inflatable thermal blanket. The patent claimed a design that caused the inflated blanket to "self-erect" into a Quonset hut-like shape, preventing contact of the blanket with the patient. The prosecution history of the patent showed that the applicant relinquished rights to any forced-air blanket other than a "self-erecting" convective thermal blanket. On that basis there could not be infringement of an allegedly equivalent blanket that rested on a patient and did not inflate itself into a self-supporting structure. *(Augustine Medical Inc. v. Gaymar Industries Inc.*, 181 F.3d 1291 (Fed. Cir. 1999).)

Regulatory Testing and Experimental Uses

To encourage competition and speed up the release of human health care and certain animal products, patent law allows companies to engage in activities that would otherwise be considered infringement if those activities were necessary for regulatory approval. If this were not available, a competitor waiting for government approval would not be able to release its product until years after a patent expires, effectively extending the patent owner's period of exclusivity.

Reverse Doctrine of Equivalents

A rarely used defense is known as the "reverse doctrine of equivalents" or "negative doctrine of equivalents." Under this defense, even if there is a literal infringement, the court will excuse the defendant's conduct if the infringing device has a different function or result than the patented invention.

Patent Misuse

A patent owner who has misused a patent cannot sue for infringement. Common examples of misuse are violations of the antitrust laws or unethical business practices. For example, if a patent owner conspired to fix the price of the patented item, this would violate antitrust laws. If the patent owner later sued for infringement, the defendant could argue that the owner is prohibited from suing because it has misused its patent rights.

Tying is a form of patent misuse in which, as a condition of a transaction, the buyer of a patented device must also purchase an additional product. For example, in one case, a company had a patent on a machine that deposited salt tablets in canned food. Purchasers of the machine were also required to buy salt tablets from the patent owner. The Supreme Court determined that the seller of the machine misused its patent rights and on that basis, was prevented from suing for infringement. (*Morton Salt Co. v. G.S. Suppiger Co.*, 314 U.S. 488 (1942).) In 1988, Congress enacted Patent Misuse Amendments that require that courts apply a "rule of reason" standard. Under the rule of reason, the court must view all the relevant factors to determine if the tying arrangement is in any way justified.

In a 2005 case, the Court of Appeals for the Federal Circuit established that there is a presumption that an antitrust violation has occurred when a company that requires the tying of products has sufficient market power. However, this presumption is considered "rebuttable" meaning that with sufficient evidence, it can always be disproved. (*Independent Ink v. Illinois Tool Works*, 396 F.3d 1342 (Fed. Cir. 2005).)

In 2010, the Federal Circuit narrowed the scope of misuse in a case involving compact disc patents. Under the Federal Circuit's new standard, there must be evidence of anticompetitive effects associated in addition to restrictions on use. Alleging wrongful conduct is not enough. (*Princo Corp. v. International Trade Commission*, 616 F.3d 1318 (Fed. Cir. 2010).)

Waiting Too Long to File the Lawsuit

Although patent law does not provide a time limit (or statute of limitations) for filing a patent infringement lawsuit, the law does state that monetary damages can be recovered only for infringements committed during the six years prior to the filing of the lawsuit. (35 U.S.C. § 286.) For example, if a patent owner sues after ten years of infringement, the owner cannot recover money damages for the first four years of infringement. In this way, the six-year limitation has become a de facto statute of limitations.

While patent law permits a patent owner to bring a lawsuit within six years of the infringement, courts do have the power to terminate lawsuits before then, under a principle known as "laches" (an equitable principle that it's unfair to proceed with a lawsuit when one party has waited an unreasonable amount of time to bring the claim). It's a bit of a fluid area, however. In one recent case, the patent owner's claim was brought within six years of infringement, and the lawsuit was dismissed based on laches. But on appeal, the Supreme Court held that laches could not bar a patent claim brought within the statute of limitations. (*SCA Hygiene Products Aktiebolag v. First Quality Baby Products, LLC*, 136 S. Ct. 1824 (2017).)

Defense to Method Claim Infringement

The patent laws were amended in 1999 to provide a defense that applies only to method claim patents. These patent claims cover methods of accomplishing a process, for example, the series of steps required for a software program to calculate a mutual fund investment. Anyone who created and used a process commercially at least one year before the filing date of a method claims patent has a full defense to a charge of infringement. If the defendant sold a product produced by the method before the patent's effective filing date, this will generally invalidate the patent.

Prior Commercial Use

Suppose your patent covers an invention that is a process, or is a machine, manufacture, or composition of matter that is used in a manufacturing or other commercial process. And suppose you find an infringer who has used the invention in the United States commercially, or transferred a useful end result of the commercial use over one year before either (a) your patent's filing date, or (b) the date you disclosed the invention to the public. In either of these cases, the alleged infringer has a complete defense to any claim of infringement of your patent, provided the infringer can prove the defense by clear and convincing evidence.

The Accidental Tourist

Suppose a French airplane lands in the United States using a navigational device that is an unauthorized copy of a similar device covered by a U.S. patent. Infringement? No, because U.S. patent law permits "temporary or accidental" stops by foreign airplanes or ships containing infringing inventions, provided that the invention is used exclusively for the needs of the transporting vessel.

CAUTION

Frivolous and fraudulent defenses. A defense should only be asserted if the defendant has a good-faith belief that it is applicable. A defense that is completely without merit, or based upon untrue facts, can destroy the defendant's credibility and result in sanctions or imprisonment stemming from felony perjury.

Ending Disputes Without a Lawsuit

The American Intellectual Property Law Association (AIPLA) estimates the median cost of patent infringement actions for a case with less than $1,000,000 in damages is $250,000 to get through discovery, and a total of $700,000 to get to a jury decision. With more than $25,000,000 at risk, those figures jump to $3,000,000 to $5,000,000 for a jury decision.

Settlement

It is possible that the infringer may wish to avoid litigation, or if litigation has started, to end it before trial. There are several advantages to a negotiated settlement:

- It saves money because there are no costs for litigation.
- It saves time compared to the two to three years required for litigation.
- It is a guaranteed payment, unlike a court judgment that must be collected and enforced.

Because of these advantages a patent owner may accept less money in settlement than might be demanded in a court case. When negotiating a settlement, the patent owner must consider the likelihood of prevailing in a federal court and any resulting award of damages. Sometimes, a patent owner will forgo payment of damages in exchange for the infringer's agreement to halt infringement. In other cases, the patent owner may agree to permit continued manufacture or sale provided the infringer pays a royalty for all past and future sales. This is sometimes referred to as a "reverse license."

A settlement is a contract signed by both parties, usually executed at the time one party pays the other. Some states have requirements regarding settlement agreements and specific language must be included to protect the rights of the parties. Sometimes, the terms of the settlement are presented in a document that is filed with the court in a form known as a stipulated judgment.

Alternative Dispute Resolution

Many disputes regarding intellectual property rights are resolved privately through informal procedures known as mediation and arbitration. Mediation is a procedure in which the parties submit their dispute to an impartial mediator who assists the parties in reaching a settlement.

Arbitration can be used if mediation is not successful. It is the referral of a dispute to one or more impartial persons, usually for a final and binding decision. Disputes regarding patent ownership or infringement involve technical and scientific issues and the parties may desire to have the matter decided by a person versed in the subject matter. In addition, the expense of patent litigation disfavors smaller entities. For these reasons, arbitration of patent disputes is encouraged and sanctioned by law. (35 U.S.C. § 294.) The American Arbitration Association has established special Patent Arbitration Rules and has gathered a national panel of patent arbitrators. International arbitration disputes are often resolved through the International Chamber of Commerce in Stockholm or the London Court of Arbitration in England. Arbitration can be initiated by an agreement or by submission of the parties.

IPRs and the Reexamination Process

The PTO can be asked to reexamine any in-force patent to determine whether prior art newly called to its attention knocks out one or more of the patent's claims—that is, to determine its validity. This may help the patent owner under some circumstances. For example, an infringer informs the patent owner of prior art that the infringer feels invalidates one or more claims in the patent. The patent owner (or the infringer or any "person who is not the owner of a patent" (15 U.S.C. § 311)) can request a reexamination by the PTO in light of the prior art and the PTO can issue either a certificate of patentability or unpatentability. This certificate can have a powerful effect on bringing the parties to a settlement.

This type of administrative hearing, brought at the PTO, is less expensive, less formal, and faster than challenging a patent owner in court. In addition, decisions are rendered by technical specialists, not juries.

The The Director of the USPTO can authorize an IPR only if "there is a reasonable likelihood that the petitioner would prevail with respect to at least one of the claims challenged in the petition." Such proceedings are limited to challenges for novelty and nonobviousness— that is, to issues relating to Sections 102 and 103 of the patent law. These claims can only be based on prior art consisting of patents and printed publications and must be filed nine months after the patent issued. Patent law also establishes many additional technical and procedural rules, generally making it more difficult to bring IPRs.

In 2017, the Supreme Court held that the USPTO has the final say as to whether to institute an IPR—that is, the decision as to whether or not to institute an IPR is not appealable. The Supreme Court also held that the USPTO's "broadest reasonable interpretation" (BRI) standard was a "reasonable exercise of the rulemaking authority that Congress delegated to the Patent Office." (*Cuozzo Speed Technologies, LLC v. Lee*, 136 S.Ct. 2131 (2016).)

The current IPR law was instituted on September 16, 2012 (following adoption of the America Invents Act (AIA)) and there have been several court decisions clarifying the IPR rules including the following:

- **IPR patent challenges are constitutional.** The Supreme Court ruled, in a 7-2 decision, that post-grant challenges to patent validity do not violate the Fifth Amendment's "taking" prohibition. The holding, which supported the Patent Trial and Appeal Board's (PTAB's) decision-making power, effectively concluded that patents are a government franchise, not necessarily a property right. (*Oil States Energy v. Greene's Energy Group*, 138 S.Ct. 1365 (2018).)

- **The CAFC okays IPRs for pre-AIA patents.** In *Celgene Corp. v. Peter*, the CAFC held "that the retroactive application of IPR proceedings to pre-AIA patents is not an unconstitutional taking under the Fifth Amendment." In other words, it is constitutional to maintain an IPR proceeding for pre-March 18, 2013 patents. (*Celgene Corp. v. Peter*, Nos. 2018-1167-1171 (CAFC (2019).)

- **The PTAB must determine the patentability of all of petitioner's disputed claims.** In a 5-4 decision, the Supreme Court held that when the PTAB initiates an IPR, it must resolve the patentability of all of the claims the petitioner has questioned. In other words, "the PTAB must address every claim the petitioner has challenged," and cannot "partially institute" an IPR review. (*SAS Institute Inc. v. Iancu*, 138 S.Ct. 1348 (2018).)

- **The CAFC determines real party in interest for IPRs.** The CAFC ruled that the PTAB applied an improper standard when determining the real party in interest for the purposes of instituting IPR proceedings. The CAFC held that "[T]he focus of the real-party-in-interest inquiry is on the patentability of the claims challenged in the IPR petition, bearing in mind who will benefit from having those claims canceled or invalidated." (*Applications in Internet Time v. RPX Corporation*, 897 F.3d 1336 (2018).)

- **The CAFC rules against tribal sovereign immunity in IPRs.** Allergen, a drug company, transferred patents to a Native American tribe and then claimed sovereign immunity to avoid an attack on its patents. ("Sovereign immunity" prevents the government or its political agencies from being sued without its consent.) The CAFC ruled that tribal sovereign immunity cannot be asserted to end IPR proceedings. (*St. Regis Mohawk Tribe v. Mylan Pharmaceuticals*, 896 F.3d 1322 (2018).)

- **No sovereign immunity for state governments in IPR proceedings.** A state university argued that its patents could not be challenged in an IPR proceeding because of sovereign immunity (see above). The CAFC disagreed, holding that sovereign immunity did not apply in USPTO enforcement actions. (*Regents of the Univ. of Minn. v. LSI Corp.*, 2018-1559, 2019 U.S. App. LEXIS 17887 (Fed. Cir. 2019).)

- **The federal government is not a "person" for purposes of IPRs.** The three types of administrative patent reviews provided by the AIA—inter partes reviews, post-grant reviews, and covered business method reviews—are available to any "person" who wants to challenge a patent's validity. At issue was whether a government agency qualified as a person. In a 6-3 decision, the Supreme Court followed precedent and held that the government was not a person for purposes of the AIA. *Return Mail v. U.S. Postal Service*, 139 S.Ct. 1853 (2019).

International Patent Law

I n this chapter, we explore basic principles of international patent law. Our perspective is through the eyes of the U.S. inventor. Because U.S. patent rights do not extend beyond national borders, American inventors who want to prevent foreign infringements must apply for patent rights in other countries. When applying, they rely on reciprocal patent filing rules that are part of international agreements (or treaties). These agreements provide consistent treatment for inventors in member nations. The three most important treaties that affect the rights of U.S. inventors are the Paris Convention, the Patent Cooperation Treaty (PCT), and the European Patent Convention (EPC). We'll discuss these treaties and we'll also cover patent rights in nations that are not members of patent treaties.

Introduction to Foreign Patent Treaties and Laws

The owner of a U.S. patent can stop anyone from making, using, selling, importing, or offering for sale any product incorporating the invention in the United States. However, U.S. patent rights stop at the American border. An inventor cannot use a U.S. patent to stop someone from making, selling, or using the invention in another country. To do that, American inventors must acquire patent rights in that country and rely on rules of reciprocity in international treaties. "Reciprocity" or "reciprocal treatment" means that when an inventor from Country A applies for a patent in Country B, the inventor will be treated in virtually the same manner as inventors living in Country B. This reciprocal treatment extends only to inventors who live in nations that have signed the treaty ("signatory nations").

Patent Treaties

The United States is a signatory nation to several international patent treaties, the most important of which are the Paris Convention and the Patent Cooperation Treaty. A list of nations that are members of each treaty is provided in Figs. 9A and 9B at the end of this chapter. The most popular jurisdictions for foreign filing are shown in bold. Below we provide a short synopsis of each treaty and we will provide more detail in subsequent sections.

Paris Convention

The United States, like the majority of industrialized nations, is a party to the Paris Convention, an international treaty that provides reciprocal patent filing rights. Members of the Paris Convention are known as Convention countries. In order to acquire patent rights, the inventor must separately file a patent application in each Convention country or group of countries (such as the European Patent Convention) that are members of the Paris Convention. The advantage of the Paris Convention for a U.S. inventor is that the inventor's filing date can be retained in another Convention country provided that the patent application is filed in the country within one year of the U.S. filing date (or six months for design patents). For example, Roberta files her U.S. patent application on May 1 2021. If Roberta files a patent application in Canada before May 1, 2022 and she claims "priority" of her U.S. application, she will have priority over any other patents that may have been filed in Canada after May 1, 2021.

CAUTION

Patent filing in non-Convention countries. A U.S. inventor filing in non-Convention countries must file the foreign application before publishing or selling the invention. This is because, unlike the United States, virtually no foreign country provides a one-year grace period (see Chapter 2). Thus, any publication or sale of the invention before filing in a non-Convention country is fatal in foreign countries.

Patent Cooperation Treaty (PCT)

Most industrialized countries are also members of the PCT, a treaty that enables inventors to file a relatively economical international application in their home country within one year of their home country filing date. There are two advantages in filing a PCT application: The inventor obtains a filing date that is good in every member country in which the inventor seeks patent protection, and an initial international patent search will be conducted (with PCT member countries relying heavily on this search). The inventor in a PCT nation must eventually file separate "national" applications in each country or group of countries (such as the EPO) where the inventor wants coverage, but the initial search procedure simplifies the international patent process.

A U.S. inventor cannot file a foreign patent application until the inventor gets a PCT foreign filing license or until six months have elapsed from the inventor's U.S. filing date. The inventor can then wait until 30 months after the U.S. filing date to file in countries that belong to the PCT. In the following sections we will discuss these treaties and related international rules in more detail.

The High Cost of Foreign Patent Filings

Patent prosecution and practice in other countries is relatively complicated and extremely expensive. It is usually only worthwhile for U.S. inventors to file applications in a foreign country where a significant market for the invention is very likely to exist, or where the inventor has a foreign licensee (someone who's paying the inventor for the invention and know-how). Otherwise, the cost of acquiring foreign patent protection may exceed the potential returns from sales of the invention. The fact that an infringement occurs in a country does not always justify filing in that country. Usually, it pays to file only if the infringement is substantial enough to justify the expense of filing, getting, and maintaining the patent, and the uncertainties of licensing and litigation.

Europatents: The European Patent Convention (EPC)

Most European nations are parties to the European Economic Community (EEC) and are also members of a treaty known as the European Patent Convention (EPC).

The Patent Laws of Other Countries Are Different

Despite the Paris Convention and other treaties covering patent applications—and except for Canada, whose patent laws and practice are practically identical to ours—almost all countries have some differences from the United States in their substantive patent laws and practices. These differences have been reduced in recent years, but let's take a look at some that still exist.

Opposition Proceedings After Allowance

Formerly, in the United States, once an application was examined and allowed, the patent issued without any further proceedings, except that the patentee could apply to have the patent reissued with narrower or broader claims. Under current patent law, U.S. patent applications are normally published 18 months after filing to allow anyone to cite prior art against the application. This is similar to, but less adversarial than the opposition proceeding in most foreign countries, under which the application is published so that anyone who believes the invention isn't patentable can cite additional prior art to the patent office and usually have a hearing in order to block the patent. After the patent issues, most foreign countries do not have any procedure for invalidating the patent aside from an infringement lawsuit, but the United States now has several post-grant review proceedings, including post-grant review, ex parte reexamination, and inter partes reexamination.

No Novelty Examination

Many smaller countries (for example, Belgium and Portugal) don't conduct novelty examinations on applications that are filed there directly (not through the European Patent Office—EPO). Instead, they simply issue a patent on every application filed and leave it up to the courts (in the event of an infringement) to determine whether the invention was novel and nonobvious.

Payment of Maintenance Fees Before Issuance of Foreign Patent

Some jurisdictions (for example, the EPO, France, Germany, Italy, Australia, and the Netherlands) require the payment of annual maintenance fees while the application is pending. But if the inventor files in these countries (except Australia) through the EPO, no individual country fees are due until the Europatent issues and is registered in each country. However, annual EPO fees are due until the Europatent issues.

No One-Year Grace Period

The United States has a one-year grace period that allows a patent applicant or the applicant's agent to expose the invention to the public up to one year before the application was filed without loss of rights. Most foreign countries don't provide any rights to go back in this manner. Therefore, a U.S. inventor must get an effective filing date in most countries before public release or sale of the invention, unless the public release came from the inventor or the inventor's agent. The inventor can obtain an effective filing date either by actually filing abroad or by filing in the United States and then filing a corresponding application in Convention countries within one year. Some countries allow an exhibit at a recognized trade show, provided the patent application is filed in that country within six months of the exhibit or trade show.

Expenses and Difficulties in the Japanese Patent Process

In Japan, the filing and translation fees are very high. Then, examination must be separately requested within seven years, requiring another stiff fee. After examination is requested, it takes about three years before the Japanese Patent Office, which is understaffed, gets around to it. Getting the application allowed is very difficult. However, it will be given more respect than in the United States. Competitors will be far less likely to infringe or challenge it. Nevertheless, Japanese courts tend to interpret patents narrowly. Claims are not given a broad reading. The result is that it is possible to make small variations to the invention and avoid infringement.

The Early Foreign Filing License or Mandatory Six-Month Delay

Normally, after filing a U.S. application, the inventor receives a filing receipt from the PTO that permits the inventor to file abroad. This permission will usually be printed on the inventor's filing receipt as follows: "Foreign Filing License Granted 2014 Aug 9." However, if the inventor's filing receipt fails to include a foreign filing license (only inventions with possible military applications won't include the license), the inventor isn't allowed to file in foreign countries until six months following the inventor's U.S. filing date. What's the reason for this? To give the U.S. government a chance to review the inventor's application for possible classification on national security grounds.

Few inventors are affected by any of this, as most applications get the foreign filing license immediately. In any case, there is usually no good reason to file before six months after the inventor's U.S. filing. If the invention does have military applications, the inventor will not only fail to get a foreign filing license, but may receive a Secrecy Order from the PTO requiring that the inventor keep the invention secret until it's declassified. This often takes 12 years. The inventor's patent can't issue until then, but the government may compensate the inventor if it uses the invention in the meantime. The inventor can foreign file an application that is under a Secrecy Order. Nonetheless, it's complicated and requires assistance from a patent attorney experienced in this area.

Putting It Together: The Most Common Route for U.S. Inventors Seeking Foreign Patent Coverage

As noted, the cost of acquiring foreign patent protection may exceed the potential return from the sale of the invention in a country (see "The High Cost of Foreign Patent Filings," above). Inventors are advised to analyze the commercial potential of an invention within a foreign nation before seeking patent protection. The most common approach taken by U.S. inventors seeking global patent rights is detailed below; in subsequent sections we will explain each of the procedures:

1. First, file in the United States and then file in non-Convention countries before publication or sale of the invention.
2. Within one year, under the Paris Convention, file a PCT application to cover PCT countries and jurisdictions (including the EPO).
3. Select the PTO or EPO for purposes of the patent search.
4. Within 30 months of the U.S. filing date, file national applications, usually with the assistance of foreign patent agents, in the EPO and non-EPO PCT countries.

The Paris Convention and the One-Year Foreign Filing Rule

The International Convention for the Protection of Industrial Property (known as the Paris Convention or simply "the Convention") is the oldest international patent treaty. The United States is a "Convention country," as are countries of the EPO, PCT, and AIPO (the African Intellectual Property Organization). A table listing Convention countries is provided in Fig. 9A at the end of this chapter.

Treaty Members: Jurisdiction and Nations

As with many international treaties, members of the Paris Convention do not have to be an individual country, but may be an organization or group of countries. For example, the EPO is considered a separate signatory of the Paris Convention. For this reason, these treaties often refer to members as "member jurisdictions," rather than as member nations or countries.

A U.S. inventor who files a regular patent application or provisional patent application (PPA, discussed in Chapter 3), can file a patent application in any Convention country within one year of the inventor's earliest filing date (or within six months for designs). The inventor's application in the Convention country will be entitled to the filing date of the inventor's U.S. application for purposes of prior-art examinations.

EXAMPLE: Sam files a regular patent application in the United States on 1 September 2018. Within one year he files French, Spanish, German, Brazilian, and Australian patent applications and is entitled to the filing date of 1 September 2018 in these countries.

Each Convention filing must be made in the language of the country in which the coverage is sought. (In the EPO, a U.S. applicant can use English, regardless of the countries in which coverage is sought.) Separate filing and search fees must be paid in each country. Many members of the Paris Convention also belong to the PCT (see Fig. 9B at the end of this chapter). Filing patent applications in countries that belong to both the Paris Convention and the PCT is generally easier than filing in non-PCT Convention countries.

If the inventor fails to file any foreign applications within the one-year period, the inventor can still file after the one-year period in any foreign countries, provided the inventor hasn't sold, published, or patented the invention yet.

However, missing the Convention's one-year deadline will result in:

- The inventor's foreign application won't be entitled to the filing date of the inventor's original application.
- Any such late application won't get the benefit of the inventor's original U.S. filing date, so any relevant prior art that has been published in the meantime can be applied against the inventor's application.

Other International Treaties

There are three other international treaties with rules similar to the Paris Convention. Members of these treaties have reciprocal priority rights in each other's countries. For example, the United States has entered into treaties with the Republic of China (Taiwan), India, and Thailand. Inventors who file a U.S. application can file patent applications in each of these countries within one year and obtain the benefit of their U.S. filing date, and vice versa. Members of these treaties are listed in Fig. 9B at the end of this chapter.

Filing in Non-Convention Countries

Fig. 9B identifies countries that are not members of the Paris Convention. U.S. inventors can file in these countries at any time, provided both of the following apply:

- The invention hasn't yet become publicly known, either by the inventor's publication, by patenting, by public sale, or by normal publication, in the course of prosecution in a foreign country.
- The inventor has been given a foreign-filing license on the inventor's U.S. filing receipt or six months have elapsed from the inventor's U.S. filing date.

> **CAUTION**
> **Don't miss the one-year filing deadline.** If the inventor misses the one-year Paris Convention deadline and the PTO subsequently issues the U.S. patent, it's too late to file a foreign application *anywhere!* The inventor will acquire patent rights only in the United States.

The Patent Cooperation Treaty (PCT)

The PCT is administered by the World Intellectual Property Organization (WIPO) in Geneva. Under the Patent Cooperation Treaty (PCT), the inventor can file a patent application in the United States and then file a single "international application" (the "PCT application") with the PCT Department of the PTO that establishes a filing date for all member countries. This filing does not result in a universal PCT patent; the inventor must eventually file separate or "national" applications in each PCT jurisdiction. However, the PCT application provides the following advantages:

- By filing one PCT application, the inventor obtains a filing date that is good in every member country in which the inventor seeks patent protection.
- An initial international patent search will be conducted by the PTO or the EPO (the inventor makes the designation) on the PCT application, and member countries will rely heavily on this search. This saves a great deal of expense and delay that would result if separate searches were conducted in each country. This search lets the inventor know what prior art is likely to be used in the actual examination process in Chapter II (see next paragraph) or in the national stage.
- The inventor may elect to have an examination performed in the PTO or EPO, depending on whether the applicant elects a process known as "Chapter II" within 22 months from the U.S. filing date or three months from transmittal of the search report. This examination differs from the search in that the PTO or EPO will actually indicate that claims are allowable or rejectable on the cited prior art.

If the inventor desires patent coverage in a PCT jurisdiction, the PCT application must be translated for non-English-speaking jurisdictions when the inventor enters the national stage. (The application can be filed in the EPO in English.) It must be filed in the foreign jurisdiction within 30 months after the inventor's U.S. filing date.

After filing the PCT application, the inventor will receive a "search report" from either the PTO or EPO depending on which is elected by the applicant. The inventor can then amend the claims once and submit a brief statement responding to any issues raised by the report. The inventor will not receive any formal indication of allowability (or rejection) from the examiner unless the inventor enters optional Chapter II of the PCT.

Before 30 months (whether or not the application is allowed or rejected), the inventor can file a national-stage application in any PCT jurisdiction. Each of the separate countries and the EPO will rely to a great extent on the international examination given by the PCT's International Bureau or the EPO. A list of the PCT jurisdictions is given in Fig. 9B. All PCT members are members of the Paris Convention, but not vice versa.

TIP

For additional assistance filing a PCT application, consult *Patent It Yourself,* by attorney David Pressman (Nolo), or review *The PCT Applicant's Guide* from the PCT Department of the PTO, the PCT section of the PTO's website, or the WIPO site (www.wipo.int). Information regarding a country's patent laws may be obtained from the country's consulate office in the United States.

Preparing an International Application Under the PCT

To file a PCT application, the inventor prepares the original U.S. application and drawings on—or so that they will fit on—A4 size paper. (The PCT application can be filed via the Internet in the PTO so no actual paper copies are ever needed.) The main differences between the PCT and U.S. national formats (both of which are acceptable for U.S. applications) are the drawing size and margins. (The standards are detailed in Chapter 5.)

In addition to the PCT application, a "Request" form (PTO PCT/ RO/101) and a "transmittal letter" (Form PTO 1382) are required. Both forms are available on the PTO website, www.uspto.gov. WIPO has software ("PCT-Easy") that enables an applicant to pay reduced fees and automate the process of completing PCT filing forms. Visit the WIPO website (www.wipo.int/portal/en/index.html) for more information.

It is advisable to file the PCT application at least a month before the anniversary of the inventor's U.S. filing date. However, the inventor can file the PCT application online via EFS-Web, or mail the PCT application as late as the last day of the one-year period from the inventor's U.S. filing date if the inventor uses Express Mail and completes the Express Mail Certification on page one of the transmittal letter.

The inventor will receive a filing receipt and separate serial number for the international PCT application. The application will eventually be transmitted for filing to the countries (including the EPO) designated on the inventor's request form. If the inventor makes any minor errors in the PCT application, the PCT Department of the PTO will give the inventor a month to correct them. When the inventor receives the PCT search report (either from the PTO or EPO), the inventor can comment on it and amend the inventor's claims once if desired, but no extended prosecution or negotiation is permitted.

Chapter II of the PCT

Within 22 months from the U.S. filing date or three months from transmittal of the search report, the inventor can elect Chapter II. This requires selecting either the PTO or the EPO to examine the application. If the inventor selects the EPO to do the examination, the inventor must file the papers with the EPO in Munich and pay the fee in euros. The inventor will receive an examination report indicating which claims will actually be allowed or rejected. The inventor can amend the application once and even interview the inventor's examiner.

National Filings Under the PCT

The inventor must file a national application in each country or jurisdiction in the inventor's PCT application within 30 months from the inventor's U.S. filing date. As mentioned, each of the separate countries and the EPO will rely to a great extent on the international examination received as part of the PCT process. In most cases, this examination will be based upon the EPO patent search or adopted from the U.S. patent search. This is one advantage of the PCT approach because the inventor saves money and time by not having to separately and fully prosecute an application in each country in which the inventor elected to file. However the inventor must hire and file through a foreign patent agent who is licensed in each country or jurisdiction in which the inventor chooses to file.

Filing in Non-PCT Convention Countries

If a U.S. inventor desires to file in a Convention country that is not a member of the PCT, the inventor must use a patent agent, a patent expert licensed to file under that non-Convention country's patent laws. The requirements vary from country to country, but drawings in the A4 size will always be needed. The inventor's foreign agent can prepare these or the inventor can have these prepared by companies that make drawings for U.S. divisional applications (see Chapter 6).

The foreign agent will require a power of attorney (sometimes notarized) and a certified copy of the inventor's U.S. application that can be obtained from the PTO. The cost for filing a foreign application in each individual country is about $1,500 to $8,000, depending on the country, the length of the inventor's application, and whether a translation is required.

> ⊘ **CAUTION**
>
> **Don't procrastinate.** A U.S. inventor should make foreign filing decisions and take action about two or three months before the end of any of the filing periods described in this chapter. This is to give the inventor and the foreign agents time to prepare (or have prepared) the necessary correspondence and translations and to order a certified copy, if needed, of the inventor's U.S. application. Although the inventor shouldn't wait until the very end of the one-year period, the inventor also shouldn't file until near the end, because there's no advantage in filing early, unless the inventor needs an early patent—for example, because the inventor is concerned about ongoing foreign infringements.

European Patent Office (EPO)

The European Patent Office (EPO) is a trilingual patent office in Munich, Germany, and The Hague, Netherlands, created as a result of a treaty known as the European Patent Convention (EPC). The EPO grants "Europatents" that are good in all member countries. An inventor can make one patent filing in the EPO and if a Europatent is issued, the patentee can then register and file translations of the patent in whatever individual member countries the patentee has selected. The patent office in each EPC country does not have to review the application separately. Unless the inventor is a resident of one of the EPO member countries, the inventor must file in the EPO via a European patent agent.

There is an additional advantage for filing at the EPO. The European Patent Convention is considered the same as a single country (a jurisdiction) under the Paris Convention and the PCT. Therefore, a U.S. inventor can file at the EPO and the effective filing date will be the same as the inventor's original U.S. filing date (provided the application is filed within the one-year foreign filing rule discussed above).

Although quite rigorous, the examination procedure at the EPO is generally smoother than the PTO because the examiners are better trained (all speak and write three languages fluently) and because they take the initiative to suggest how to write the inventor's claims to get them allowed. The EPO application is published for opposition 18 months after filing. During the pendency of the EPO application, annual maintenance fees must be paid to the EPO.

If the inventor's application is allowed, the inventor is granted a Europatent that lasts for 20 years from the inventor's filing date (provided the inventor pays maintenance fees in the selected member countries). The patent is automatically valid in each member country of the EPC that is designated in the inventor's application, provided that the inventor registers, files translations, appoints an agent, and pays maintenance fees in each country. All member countries of the EPO are indicated in Fig. 9B, below.

There are some drawbacks for U.S. inventors. Filing in the EPO is very expensive and requires payment of an annuity to the EPO each year the inventor's application is on file there, until the Europatent issues. If the inventor registers the patent in any EPC member country, the inventor must pay annuities in that country.

Locating Foreign Patent Agents

U.S. inventors who want to file abroad will probably need to find a foreign patent agent who's familiar with patent prosecution in the countries where protection is desired. In most countries, patent professionals are called "agents" rather than "attorneys." As in the United States, foreign agents are licensed to represent clients before their patent office, but not their courts.

The best way to find foreign agents is by conducting an Internet search for suitable patent agents. Almost all now have websites, which can be located easily by using search terms like "Japanese patent agents."

Another method of locating a foreign agent is through a U.S. patent attorney (see Chapter 10) because most attorneys are associated with one or more patent agents in other countries.

Names of agents can also be located:

- in the telephone directory of the city where the patent office of the foreign country is located
- at the consulate of the country (most foreign countries have consulates in major U.S. cities), and
- for filing in Europe, we recommend either hiring a British or a German firm of patent agents. Most British agents are in London and many German agents are in Munich. Although perhaps not as fluent in English as their British counterparts, the German agents have the compensating advantage of their physical proximity to the EPO. All patent agents who are licensed to practice before the EPO are listed on the EPO's website at www.epo.org.

CAUTION

Foreign patent agents. Always try to get several references or a referral regarding any foreign patent agent you are contemplating hiring. At the very least, get background information on the agent, such as the names of schools attended, degrees awarded, licenses held, representative clients and patents prosecuted, years in business, and so on. In addition, seek a written estimate of the expected costs. Some foreign patent agents, like some U.S. patent attorneys and agents, are not competent or are inclined to overcharge.

Members of the Paris Convention

Afghanistan	**Canada**	**Germany**
Albania	Central African Republic	Ghana
Algeria	Chad	Greece
Andorra	Chile	Grenada
Angola	China	Guatemala
Antigua and Barbuda	Colombia	Guinea
Argentina	Comoros	Guinea-Bissau
Armenia	Congo	Guyana
Australia	Costa Rica	Haiti
Austria	Côte d'Ivoire	Holy See
Azerbaijan	Croatia	Honduras
Bahamas	Cuba	Hungary
Bahrain	Cyprus	Iceland
Bangladesh	Czech Republic	India
Barbados	Dem. People's Rep. of Korea	Indonesia
Belarus	Dem. Rep. of Congo	Iran
Belgium	Denmark	Iraq
Belize	Djibouti	Ireland
Benin	Dominica	Israel
Bhutan	Dominican Republic	Italy
Bolivia	Ecuador	Jamaica
Bosnia and Herzegovina	Egypt	**Japan**
Botswana	El Salvador	Jordan
Brazil	Equatorial Guinea	Kazakhstan
Brunei	Estonia	Kenya
Bulgaria	Finland	Kuwait
Burkina Faso	**France**	Kyrgyzstan
Burundi	Gabon	Lao People's Dem. Rep.
Cambodia	Gambia	Latvia
Cameroon	Georgia	Lebanon

Figure 9A—Members of the Paris Convention

Members of the Paris Convention (continued)

Lesotho	Panama	Sri Lanka
Liberia	Papua New Guinea	Sudan
Libya	Paraguay	Suriname
Liechtenstein	Peru	Swaziland
Lithuania	Philippines	Sweden
Luxembourg	Poland	Switzerland
Madagascar	Portugal	Syrian Arab Republic
Malawi	Qatar	Tajikistan
Malaysia	Republic of Korea	Thailand
Mali	Republic of Moldova	Togo
Malta	Romania	Tonga
Mauritania	Russian Federation	Trinidad and Tobago
Mauritius	Rwanda	Tunisia
Mexico	Saint Kitts and Nevis	Turkey
Monaco	Saint Lucia	Turkmenistan
Mongolia	St. Vincent & Grenadines	Uganda
Montenegro	Samoa	Ukraine
Morocco	San Marino	United Arab Emirates
Mozambique	São Tomé and Príncipe	**United Kingdom**
Namibia	Saudi Arabia	United Rep. of Tanzania
Nepal	Senegal	**United States**
Netherlands	Serbia	Uruguay
New Zealand	Seychelles	Uzbekistan
Nicaragua	Sierra Leone	Venezuela
Niger	Singapore	Vietnam
Nigeria	Slovakia	Yemen
Norway	Slovenia	Zambia
Oman	South Africa	Zimbabwe
Pakistan	Spain	

Figure 9A—Members of the Paris Convention (continued)

Members of the Patent Cooperation Treaty

Albania	Chile	**Germany**
Algeria	China	Ghana
Angola	Colombia	Greece
Antigua and Barbuda	Comoros	Grenada
Argentina	Congo	Guatemala
Armenia	Costa Rica	Guinea
Australia	Côte d'Ivoire	Guinea-Bissau
Austria	Croatia	Holy See
Azerbaijan	Cuba	Honduras
Bahrain	Cyprus	Hungary
Barbados	Czech Republic	Iceland
Belarus	Dem. People's Rep. of Korea	India
Belgium	Denmark	Indonesia
Belize	Djibouti	Iran
Benin	Dominica	Ireland
Bosnia and Herzegovina	Dominican Republic	Israel
Botswana	Ecuador	Italy
Brazil	Egypt	**Japan**
Brunei	El Salvador	**Jordan**
Bulgaria	Equatorial Guinea	Kazakhstan
Burkina Faso	Estonia	Kenya
Cambodia	Finland	Kyrgyzstan
Cameroon	**France**	Lao People's Dem. Republic
Canada	Gabon	Latvia
Central African Republic	Gambia	Lesotho
Chad	Georgia	Liberia

Figure 9B—Memberships in Patent Conventions

Members of the Patent Cooperation Treaty (continued)

Libya	Peru	Spain
Liechtenstein	Philippines	Sri Lanka
Lithuania	Poland	Sudan
Luxembourg	Portugal	Swaziland
Madagascar	Qatar	Sweden
Malawi	Republic of Korea	Switzerland
Malaysia	Republic of Moldova	Syrian Arab Republic
Mali	Romania	Tajikistan
Malta	Russian Federation	Thailand
Mauritania	Rwanda	Former Yugoslav Rep. of Macedonia
Mexico	Saint Kitts and Nevis	
Monaco	Saint Lucia	Togo
Mongolia	Samoa	Trinidad and Tobago
Montenegro	St. Vincent & Grenadines	Tunisia
Morocco	San Marino	Turkey
Mozambique	São Tomé and Príncipe	Turkmenistan
Namibia	Saudi Arabia	Uganda
Netherlands	Senegal	Ukraine
New Zealand	Serbia	United Arab Emirates
Nicaragua	Seychelles	**United Kingdom**
Niger	Sierra Leone	United Rep. of Tanzania
Nigeria	Singapore	**United States**
Norway	Slovakia	Uzbekistan
Panama	Slovenia	Vietnam
Papua New Guinea	South Africa	Zambia
		Zimbabwe

Figure 9B—Memberships in Patent Conventions (continued)

Member States of the European Patent Convention

Albania	Iceland	Poland
Austria	Ireland	Portugal
Belgium	Italy	Romania
Bulgaria	Latvia	San Marino
Croatia	Liechtenstein	Serbia
Cyprus	Lithuania	Slovakia
Czech Republic	Luxembourg	Slovenia
Denmark	Macedonia (Former Yugoslav Rep. of)	Spain
Finland		Sweden
France	Malta	Switzerland
Germany	Monaco	Turkey
Greece	Netherlands	**United Kingdom**
Hungary	Norway	

Figure 9B—Memberships in Patent Conventions (continued)

Help Beyond This Book

H opefully, this book provides all the basic information you will need. However, you may find yourself in a complicated situation that requires additional research or professional advice from a patent attorney or another expert. If you do have to get outside help, we provide other resources in this chapter.

First, we direct you to useful sources of more information for inventors. Next, we point you to additional trustworthy resources on patents and intellectual property law. Finally, we offer guidance on working with attorneys.

Inventor Resources

The following is a list of inventor resources, including organizations, bookstores, and websites with particular information on patents and other intellectual property issues:

- **Inventors' Digest (www.inventorsdigest.com).** The *Inventors' Digest* and its accompanying website publish information for independent inventors at a subscription rate of $42/year for six issues. It includes articles on new inventions, licensing and marketing, as well as advertisements from reputable inventor promotion companies.
- **National Inventor Fraud Center (www.inventorfraud.com).** This organization reports on fraud by invention marketing companies.
- **PTO Inventor & Entrepreneur Resources (www.uspto.gov/learning-and-resources/inventors-entrepreneurs-resources).** This is a PTO portal aimed at providing services and support to entrepreneurs and independent inventors.
- **Ronald J. Riley's Inventor Resources (www.inventored.org).** This website provides comprehensive links and advice for inventors.
- **InventNET (www.inventnet.com).** This site provides useful information and resources for inventors.
- **Global Patent/Innovation Quality (www.bustpatents.com).** A great source of information on patents and patent practices by one of the PTO's most vocal critics. Also offers a free newsletter.
- **IPWatchdog (www.ipwatchdog.com).** One of the leading sources for news and information in the patent and innovation industries.

Patents and Intellectual Property Resources

Below are some additional sources of information on patent and intellectual property law. Many of these sources are accessible online.

Nolo Books on Intellectual Property

There is a world of intellectual property law beyond patents. If you are interested in understanding other principles of intellectual property law that may apply to your invention, Nolo (www.nolo.com), the publisher of this book, also publishes a number of other titles on intellectual property, including:

- *How to Make Patent Drawings*, by Jack Lo and David Pressman
- *Patent It Yourself*, by David Pressman
- *Patent Pending in 24 Hours*, by Richard Stim and David Pressman
- *Patent, Copyright & Trademark: An Intellectual Property Desk Reference*, by Richard Stim
- *Profit From Your Idea: How to Make Smart Licensing Deals*, by Richard Stim
- *The Copyright Handbook: What Every Writer Needs to Know*, by Stephen Fishman, and
- *Trademark: Legal Care for Your Business & Product Name*, by Stephen Fishman.

Additional Intellectual Property Resources

- **U.S. Copyright Office (www.copyright.gov).** The Copyright Office has numerous circulars, kits, and other publications.
- **Legal Information Institute (www.law.cornell.edu).** The Legal Information Institute provides intellectual property links and downloadable copies of statutes and cases.
- **U.S. Patent & Trademark Office (PTO): Patent Information (www.uspto. gov).** The PTO website offers several informational pamphlets. There is also an alphabetical and geographical listing of patent attorneys and agents registered to practice before the

PTO ("Directory of Registered Patent Attorneys and Agents Arranged by States and Countries"). The PTO also has an online searchable database of patent abstracts (short summaries of patents). For patent searching purposes, this database is an excellent and inexpensive first step in the searching procedure. Patent forms and many important publications, including *General Information About Patents, Manual of Patent Examining Procedures, Examination Guidelines for Computer-Related Inventions,* and *Rules of Practice and Patent Laws* can be downloaded from the PTO website.

- **U.S. Patent & Trademark Office (PTO): Trademark Information (www.uspto.gov/trademark).** A division of the PTO examines and maintains trademark applications.
- *The PCT Applicant's Guide*, a brochure on how to utilize the Patent Cooperation Treaty, is available for free online from the World Intellectual Property Organization (WIPO) at www.wipo.int/pct/en/appguide/index.jsp.

RESOURCE

Nolo's website (www.nolo.com) also offers an extensive Legal Encyclopedia that includes a section on intellectual property. You'll find answers to frequently asked questions about patents, copyrights, trademarks, and other related topics, as well as sample chapters of Nolo books and a wide range of articles.

Legal Research: You Can Do It

Conducting legal research is not as difficult as it may seem. Nolo publishes a basic legal research guide, *Legal Research: How to Find & Understand the Law*, written by attorney Stephen Elias and the Editors of Nolo. It walks you through the various sources of law, explains how they fit together, and shows you how to use them to answer your legal questions. *Legal Research* also directs you to legal information available on the Internet.

For detailed legal research, you will probably have to visit a local law library. In California, every county has a law library that is open to the public. If there's a public law school in your area, it probably has a law library that's open to the public. Other public law libraries are often run by local bar associations or as an adjunct to the local courts. Law libraries associated with private law schools often allow only limited public access. Call to speak with the law librarian to determine your right to access. You can always call your local bar association to find out what public law libraries are in your area.

Working With an Attorney

At some point, you may need the advice and counsel of an experienced patent attorney. Your first step is to find one in your area who can help you. All patent attorneys are listed in the PTO publication *Attorneys and Agents Registered to Practice Before the U.S. Patent and Trademark Office* (A&ARTP). It is available in many public libraries and Patent and Trademark Depository Libraries, government bookstores, and on the PTO's website (www.uspto.gov).

Reducing the Size of Your Bill

Working with a patent attorney can be expensive. You can save yourself a lot of money and grief by following this list of helpful tips as you work through your case.

Keep it short. If you pay your attorney on an hourly basis, keep your conversations short and avoid making several calls a day. Consolidate your questions so that you can ask them all in one exchange.

Get a fee agreement. We recommend that you get a written fee agreement when dealing with an attorney. Read it and understand your rights as a client. Ensure that your fee agreement gives you the right to an itemized statement along with the bill detailing the work done and time spent. Some state statutes and the state agencies that license lawyers require a written fee agreement. For example, California requires that attorneys provide a written agreement when the fee exceeds $1,000.

Review billings carefully. Your lawyer's bill should be clear. Do not accept summary billings such as the single phrase "litigation work" used to explain a block of time for which you are billed a great deal of money.

Watch out for hidden expenses. Find out what expenses you must cover. Watch out if your attorney wants to bill for services such as word processing or administrative services. This means you will be paying the secretary's salary. Also beware of fax and copying charges. Some firms charge clients per page for incoming and outgoing faxes.

Don't take litigation lightly. As a general rule, beware of litigation! If you are involved in a lawsuit, it may take months or years to resolve. Some go on for decades. It usually costs $100,000 or more and the only ones who profit are usually the lawyers. The average cost for a full-blown patent infringement can run from about $500,000 to $2,000,000. If you're in a dispute, ask your attorney about alternative dispute resolution (ADR) methods such as arbitration and mediation. Often these procedures can save money and they're faster than litigation. If those methods don't work or aren't available, ask your attorney for an assessment of your odds and the potential costs before filing a lawsuit. The assessment and underlying reasoning should be in plain English. If a lawyer can't explain your situation clearly to you, he probably won't be able to explain it clearly to a judge or jury.

The American Intellectual Property Law Association (AIPLA) may be able to assist you in locating patent attorneys in your area. Contact the AIPLA at www.aipla.org or at 2001 Jefferson Davis Highway, Suite 203, Arlington, VA 22202, phone: 703-415-0780. The Intellectual Property Law Association of the American Bar Association also has a listing of intellectual property attorneys. Contact them at www.abanet.org or at 312-988-5000.

Nolo (www.nolo.com), the publisher of this book, also provides a lawyer directory and related referral services that can direct you to an intellectual property lawyer near you.

Most attorneys bill on an hourly basis ($150 to $600 an hour) and send a bill at the end of each month. Some attorneys bill on a fixed fee basis (for example, $1,200 for a patentability search, $2,000 for a patent validity opinion, and $6,000 for a simple patent application).

CAUTION

In many states, such as California, clients always have the right to terminate their relationships with an attorney, although this does not terminate the obligation to pay the attorney. If you don't respect and trust your attorney's professional abilities, you should switch and find a new attorney. Under most state bar rules, your attorney is required to deliver all of your papers to you at your request and without charge upon termination. However, you should not make this decision hastily. Switching attorneys is a nuisance, and you may lose time and money.

Glossary

Abandonment. 1. Allowing a pending, active patent application to be removed from the PTO's active files and treated as if the inventor has given up all claims to a patent on the invention. An inventor can expressly abandon an application by letter or allow an application to go abandoned by not timely replying to an office action. 2. Treating an invention as if the inventor has lost all interest in exploiting it, usually by not developing it or by not filing a patent application on it for a very long time.

Abstract. A concise, one-paragraph summary of the patent. It details the structure, nature, and purpose of the invention. The abstract is used by the PTO and the public to quickly determine the gist of what is being disclosed.

Actual damages (also known as compensatory damages). In a lawsuit, money awarded to one party to cover actual injury or economic loss. Actual damages are intended to put the injured party in the position he or she was in prior to the injury.

Answer. A written response to a complaint (the opening papers in a lawsuit) in which the defendant admits or denies the allegations and may provide a list of defenses.

Article. (see **Manufacture**).

Best mode. The inventor's principal and preferred method of embodying the invention.

Cease and desist letter. Correspondence from the owner of a proprietary work that requests the cessation of all infringing activity.

Clear and convincing proof. Evidence that is highly probable and free from serious doubt.

Complaint. Papers filed with a court clerk by the plaintiff to initiate a lawsuit by setting out facts and legal claims (usually called "causes of action").

Compositions of matter. Items such as chemical compositions, conglomerates, aggregates, or other chemically significant substances that are usually supplied in bulk (solid or particulate), liquid, or gaseous form. A composition of matter is one of the statutory classes of invention.

Confidentiality agreement (also known as a nondisclosure agreement). A contract in which one or both parties agree not to disclose certain information.

Continuation application. A new patent application that is connected to an earlier-filed ("parent") application and that allows the applicant to re-present an invention and get a second or third bite at the apple. The applicant must file the continuation while the parent application is still pending. A continuation application claims the same invention and is cross-referenced to the parent application, but usually has a new set of claims. The applicant retains the filing date of the parent application for purposes of determining the relevancy of prior art.

Continuation-in-Part (CIP). Less common than a continuation application, this form of extension application is used when a portion or all of an earlier patent application is continued and new matter (not disclosed in the earlier application) is included. CIP applications are used when an applicant wants to present an improvement but is prevented from adding a pending application to it because of the prohibition against adding "new matter."

Continuing Prosecution Application (CPA). A patent application that is like a continuation application in effect, but no new application need be filed. The applicant merely pays another filing fee, submits new claims, and files a CPA request form. CPAs can only be used for applications filed prior to 2000 May 29. Applications after that date must use the **Request for Continued Examination.**

Contributory infringement. Occurs when a material component of a patented invention is sold with knowledge that the component is designed for an unauthorized use. This type of infringement cannot occur unless there is a direct infringement. In other words, it is not enough to sell infringing parts; those parts must be used in an infringing invention.

Copyright. The legal right to exclude others, for a limited time, from copying, selling, performing, displaying, or making derivative versions of a work of authorship such as a writing, music, or artwork.

Counterclaim. A legal claim usually asserted by the defendant against an opposing party, usually the plaintiff.

Court of Appeals for the Federal Circuit (CAFC). The federal appeals court that specializes in patent appeals. If the Patent Trial and Appeal Board rejects an application appeal, an applicant can further appeal to the CAFC within 60 days of the decision. If the CAFC upholds the PTO, the applicant can request the United States Supreme Court hear the case (although the Supreme Court rarely hears patent appeals).

Declaratory relief. A request that the court sort out the rights and legal obligations of the parties in the midst of an actual controversy.

Deposit date. The date the PTO receives a patent application.

Deposition. Oral or written testimony of a party or witness and given under oath.

Derivation Hearing. As of March 2013, the USPTO permits a patent owner to bring a derivation hearing at the USPTO (replacing interference proceedings) against another patent owner claiming to have the same invention and who has an earlier effective filing date. The derivation hearing request must be filed within a one-year period beginning on the date of the first publication of a claim in the earlier filed application. Alternatively, the owner of a patent may sue the owner of another patent that claims the same invention and has an earlier effective filing date. These lawsuits can only be brought if the invention claiming priority was derived directly from the person seeking relief.

Design patent. Covers the unique, ornamental visible and nonfunctional shape or design of a nonnatural object.

Divisional application. A patent application used when an applicant wants to protect several inventions claimed in the original application. The official definition is "a later application for a distinct or independent invention, carved out of a pending application and disclosing and claiming only subject matter disclosed in the earlier or parent application." (MPEP § 201.06.) A divisional application is entitled to the filing date of the parent case for purposes of overcoming prior art. The divisional application must be filed while the parent is pending. A divisional application can be filed as a CPA.

Doctrine of Equivalents (DoE). A form of patent infringement that occurs when an invention performs substantially the same function in substantially the same manner and obtains the same result as the patented invention. A court analyzes each element of the patented invention separately. Under a recent Supreme Court decision, the DoE must be applied on an element-by-element basis to the claims.

Double patenting. When an applicant has obtained a patent and has filed a second application containing the same invention, the second application will be rejected. If the second application resulted in a patent, that patent will be invalidated. Two applications contain the same invention when the two inventions are literally the same or the second invention is an obvious modification of the first invention.

Embodiment. A physical version of an invention as described in a patent application; a patent application may describe several embodiments of an invention, but is supposed to state the one that the inventor considers the **best mode** as of the filing date (see **ramification**).

Enhanced damages (treble damages). In exceptionally egregious infringement cases, financial damages may be increased, at the discretion of the court, up to triple the award for actual damages (known as "enhanced damages").

Examiner's Answer. A brief submitted by a patent examiner in response to an applicant's brief in an appeal to the PTO's Patent Trial and Appeal Board.

Exclusive jurisdiction. The sole authority of a court to hear a certain type of case.

Exhaustion. (see **First sale doctrine**).

Ex parte (Latin: *one party only*). Refers to legal proceedings where only one party is present or represented.

File wrapper estoppel (or prosecution history estoppel). Affirmative defense used in patent infringement litigation that precludes the patent owner from asserting rights that were disclaimed during the patent application process. The term is derived from the fact that the official file in which a patent is contained at the Patent and Trademark Office is known as a "file wrapper." All statements, admissions, correspondence, or documentation relating to the invention are placed in the file wrapper. Estoppel means that a party is prevented from acting contrary to a former statement or action when someone else has relied to his detriment on the prior statement or action.

Final Office Action. The examiner's response to the applicant's first amendment. The final Office Action is supposed to end the prosecution stage but a "final action" is rarely final.

First Office Action (sometimes called an "official letter" or "OA"). Response from the patent examiner after the initial examination of the application. It is very rare that an application is allowed in the first Office Action. More often, the examiner rejects some or all of the claims.

First sale doctrine (also known as the exhaustion doctrine). Once a patented product (or product resulting from a patented process) is sold or licensed, the patent owner's rights are exhausted and the owner has no further rights as to the resale of that particular article.

Generic (genus). An entire group or class, or a group of related items or species.

Grace period. A period in which an action may be taken even though the normal period for taking action has passed.

Indirect infringement. Occurs either when someone is persuaded to make, use, or sell a patented invention without authorization (inducing infringement); or when a material component of a patented invention is sold with knowledge that the component is designed for an unauthorized use (contributory infringement). An indirect infringement cannot occur unless there is a direct infringement. In other words, it is not enough to sell infringing parts; those parts must be used in an infringing invention.

Infringement. An invention is infringing if it is covered by at least one claim of a patent or if it performs substantially the same function in substantially the same manner and obtains the same result as the claimed invention (see **Doctrine of Equivalents**).

Injunction. A court order requiring that a party halt a particular activity. In the case of patent infringement, a court can order all infringing activity be halted at the end of a trial (a permanent injunction) or the patent owner can attempt to halt the infringing activity immediately, rather than wait for a trial (a preliminary injunction). A court uses two factors to determine whether to grant a preliminary injunction: (1) Is the plaintiff likely to succeed in the lawsuit? and (2) Will the plaintiff suffer irreparable harm if the injunction is not granted? The patent owner may seek relief for a very short injunction known as a **temporary restraining order** or **TRO**, which usually only lasts a few days or weeks. A temporary restraining order may be granted without notice to the infringer if it appears that immediate damage will result—for example, that evidence will be destroyed.

Inter partes (Latin: *between parties*). Refers to legal proceedings where all parties to the action are represented.

Interrogatories. Written questions that must be answered under oath.

Invention. Any new article, machine, composition, or process or new use developed by a human.

Jury instructions. Explanations of the legal rules that the jury must use in reaching a verdict.

Lab notebook. A system of documenting an invention that usually includes descriptions of the invention and novel features; procedures used in the building and testing of the invention; drawings, photos, or sketches of the invention; test results and conclusions; discussions of any known prior-art references; and additional documentation such as correspondence and purchase receipts.

Literal infringement. Occurs if a defendant makes, sells, or uses the invention defined in the plaintiff's patent claim. In other words, the infringing product includes each and every component, part, or step in the claim. It is a literal infringement because the defendant's device is actually the same invention as in the patent claim.

Machine. A device or things used for accomplishing a task; usually involves some activity or motion performed by working parts. A machine is one of the statutory classes of invention.

Magistrate. An officer of the court who may exercise some of the authority of a federal district court judge, including the authority to conduct a jury or nonjury trial.

Manufacture (sometimes termed "article of manufacture"). An item made by human hands or by a machine; it usually has working or moving parts as prime features. A manufacture is one of the statutory classes of invention.

Means-plus-function clause (or means-for clause). A provision in a patent claim in which the applicant does not specifically describe the structure of one of the items in the patent and instead describes the function of the item. The term is derived from the fact that the clause usually starts with the word "means."

Method. (*See* **process**).

Micro entity. A patent applicant status that enables qualifying applicants to pay the lowest fees.

New matter. Any technical information, including dimensions, materials, etc., that was not present in the patent application as originally filed. An applicant can never add new matter to an application. (PTO Rule 118.)

New-use invention. A new and unobvious process or method for using an old and known invention. A new use is one of the statutory classes of invention.

Nonobviousness. A standard of patentability that requires that an invention produce "unusual and surprising results." In 1966, the U.S. Supreme Court established the steps for determining unobviousness in the case of *Graham v. John Deere*, 383 U.S. 1 (1966).

Notice of Allowance. A document issued when the examiner is convinced that the application meets the requirements of patentability. An issue fee is due within three months.

Objection. A disapproval made by an examiner to a nonsubstantive matter, such as an unclear drawing or dependent claim having a rejected claim.

Objects and advantages. A phrase used to explain "what the invention accomplishes." Usually, the objects are also the invention's advantages, since those aspects are intended to be superior over prior art.

Office Action (OA, also known as Official Letter or Examiner's Action).
Correspondence (usually including forms and a letter) from a patent
examiner that describes what is wrong with the application and
why it cannot be allowed. Generally, an OA will reject claims, list
defects in the specifications or drawings, raise objections, or cite and
enclose copies of relevant prior art demonstrating a lack of novelty or
nonobviousness.

Patent. A grant from a government that confers upon an inventor the
right to exclude others from making, using, selling, importing, or
offering an invention for sale for a fixed period of time.

Patent application. A set of papers that describe an invention and that are
suitable for filing in a patent office in order to apply for a patent on
the invention.

Patent Application Declaration (PAD). A declaration that identifies
the inventor or joint inventors and provides an attestation by the
applicant that the inventor understands the contents of the claims
and specification and has fully disclosed all material information.
The PTO provides a form for the PAD.

Patent misuse. A defense in patent infringement that prevents a patent
owner who has abused patent law from enforcing patent rights.
Common examples of misuse are violation of the antitrust laws or
unethical business practices.

Patent pending (also known as the "pendency period"). Time between filing
a patent application (or PPA) and issuance of the patent. The inventor
has no patent rights during this period. However, when and if the
patent later issues, the inventor will obtain the right to prevent the
continuation of any infringing activity that started during the pendency
period. If the application has been published by the PTO during the
pendency period and the infringer had notice, the applicant may later
seek royalties for these infringements during the pendency period.
It's a criminal offense to use the words "patent applied for" or "patent
pending" (they mean the same thing) in any advertising if there's no
active, applicable regular or provisional patent application on file.

Patent prosecution. The process of shepherding a patent application
through the Patent and Trademark Office.

Patent Rules of Practice. Administrative regulations located in Volume 37 of the Code of Federal Regulations (37 CFR § 1).

Patent Trial and Appeal Board. The America Invents Act (AIA), enacted in September 2011, replaced the Board of Patent Appeals and Interferences with the Patent Trial and Appeal Board (the Board). This change was effective as of March 16, 2013.

Pendency period. (*see* **Patent pending**).

Permanent injunction. A durable injunction issued after a final judgment on the merits of the case; permanently restrains the defendant from engaging in the infringing activity.

Petition to Make Special. An applicant can, under certain circumstances, have an application examined sooner than the normal course of PTO examination (one to three years). This is accomplished by filing a "Petition to Make Special" (PTMS), together with a Supporting Declaration.

Plant patent. Covers plants that can be reproduced through the use of grafts and cuttings (asexual reproduction).

Power of attorney. A document that gives another person legal authority to act on your behalf. If an attorney is preparing an application on behalf of an inventor, a power of attorney may be filed to formally authorize the patent attorney or agent to act on behalf of the inventor.

Prima facie (Latin: *on its face*). At first sight, obvious.

Prior art. The state of knowledge existing or publicly available before the date of filing of a patent application.

Process (sometimes referred to as a "method"). A way of doing or making things that involves more than purely mental manipulations. A process is one of the statutory classes of invention.

Provisional Patent Application (PPA). An interim document that clearly explains how to make and use the invention. The PPA is equivalent to a reduction to practice (see below). If a regular patent application is filed within one year of filing the PPA, the inventor can use the PPA's filing date for the purpose of deciding whether a reference is prior art. In addition to an early filing date, an inventor may claim patent pending status for the one-year period following the filing of the PPA.

Ramification. A version or variation of an invention that is different from a main version or **best mode**.

Reissue application. An application used to apply for a replacement patent that corrects information in a patent. It is usually filed when a patent owner believes the claims are not broad enough, the claims are too broad (the applicant discovered a new reference), or there are significant errors in the specification. In these cases, the applicant seeks to correct the patent by filing an application to get the applicant's original patent reissued at any time during its term. The reissue patent will take the place of the applicant's original patent and expire the same time as the original patent would have expired. If the applicant wants to broaden the claims of the patent through a reissue application, the applicant must do so within two years from the date the original patent issued. There is a risk in filing a reissue application because all of the claims of the original patent will be examined and can be rejected.

Rejection. A disapproval made by an examiner to a substantive matter such as a claim which is deemed obvious over the prior art.

Repair doctrine. Affirmative defense based on the right of an authorized licensor of a patented device to repair and replace unpatented components. It also includes the right to sell materials used to repair or replace a patented invention The defense does not apply for completely rebuilt inventions, unauthorized inventions, or items that are made or sold without authorization of the patent owner.

Reply. A brief submitted by a patent applicant in response to an examiner's **answer**.

Request for admission. Request for a party to the lawsuit to admit the truthfulness of a statement.

Request for Continued Examination (RCE). A paper filed when a patent applicant wishes to continue prosecuting an application that has received a final **Office Action**. Filing the RCE with another filing fee effectively removes the final action so that the applicant can submit further amendments—for example, new claims, new arguments, a new declaration, or new references.

Request for production of documents. The way a party to a lawsuit obtains documents or other physical evidence from the other side.

Reverse doctrine of equivalents (or negative doctrine of equivalents). A rarely used affirmative defense to patent infringement in which, even if there is a literal infringement, the court will excuse the defendant's conduct if the infringing device has a different function or result than the patented invention. The doctrine is applied when the allegedly infringing device performs the same function in a substantially different way.

Sequence listing. An attachment to a patent application used if a biotech invention includes a sequence listing of a nucleotide or amino acid sequence. The applicant attaches this information on separate sheets of paper and refers to the sequence listing in the application. (See PTO Rule 77.) If there is no sequence listing, the applicant states "Nonapplicable."

Small entity. A status that enables small businesses, independent inventors, and nonprofit companies to pay a reduced application fee. There are three types of small entities: (1) independent inventors, (2) nonprofit companies, and (3) small businesses. To qualify, an independent inventor must either own all rights, or have transferred—or be obligated to transfer—rights to a small business or nonprofit organization. Nonprofit organizations are defined and listed in the Code of Federal Regulations and usually are educational institutions or charitable organizations. A small-entity business is one with fewer than 500 employees. The number of employees is computed by averaging the number of full- and part-time employees during a fiscal year.

Species. One of a group of related individual items collectively subordinate to a **genus**.

Specification. A patent application disclosure made by the inventor and drafted so that an individual skilled in the art to which the invention pertains can, when reading the patent, make and use the invention without needing further experiment. A specification is constructed of several sections, including a description, claims, and an abstract. Collectively, these sections form a narrative that describes and distinguishes the invention. A statute requires that the specification disclose the best way (or **best mode**) of making and using the invention, but a failure to disclose the best mode can no longer be used to invalidate a patent.

Statute of limitations. The legally prescribed time limit in which a lawsuit must be filed. In patent law there is no time limit (statute of limitations) for filing a patent infringement lawsuit, but monetary damages can be recovered only for infringements committed during the six years prior to the filing of the lawsuit. For example, if a patent owner sues after ten years of infringement, the owner cannot recover monetary damages for the first four years of infringement. Despite the fact that there is no law setting a time limit, courts will not permit a patent owner to sue for infringement if the owner has waited an unreasonable time to file the lawsuit ("laches").

Statutory Invention Registration (SIR). A document that allows an applicant who abandons an application to prevent anyone else from getting a valid patent on the same invention. This is accomplished by converting the patent application to a SIR.

Statutory subject matter. An invention that falls into one of the statutory classes: process (method), machine, article of manufacture, composition, or a "new use" of one of the first four.

Substitute application. Essentially a duplicate of an abandoned patent application. (See MPEP § 201.09.) The disadvantage of a substitute application is that the applicant doesn't get the benefit of the filing date of the previously abandoned patent application, which could be useful, because any prior art occurring after the filing date of the earlier case can be used against the substitute case. If the applicant's substitute application issues into a patent, the patent will expire 20 years from the filing date of the substitute.

Successor liability. Responsibility for infringement that is borne by a company that has purchased another company that is liable for infringements. In order for successor liability to occur, there must be an agreement between the companies to assume liability, a merger between the companies, or the purchaser must be a "continuation" of the purchased business. If the sale is made to escape liability and lacks any of the foregoing characteristics, liability will still attach.

Summons. A document served with the **complaint** that tells the defendant he has been sued, has a certain time limit in which to respond, and must appear in court on a stated date.

Temporary restraining order (TRO). A court order that tells one party to do or stop doing something—for example to stop infringing. A TRO is issued after the aggrieved party appears before a judge. Once the TRO is issued, the court holds a second hearing where the other side can tell his story and the court can decide whether to make the TRO permanent by issuing an **injunction**. The TRO is often granted *ex parte* (without allowing the other side to respond), and for that reason is short in duration and remains in effect only until the court has an opportunity to schedule a hearing for the preliminary injunction.

Traverse. To argue against.

Tying. A form of patent misuse in which, as a condition of a transaction, the buyer of a patented device must also purchase an additional product. For example, in one case a company had a patent on a machine that deposited salt tablets in canned food. Purchasers of the machine were also required to buy salt tablets from the patent owner. A party that commits patent misuse may have its patent invalidated, may have to pay monetary damages, or both.

Utility patent. The main type of patent, which covers inventions that function in a unique manner to produce a utilitarian result.

Verified statement. A statement made under oath or a declaration. A false verified statement is punishable as perjury.

Vicarious liability. Legal responsibility that results when a business such as a corporation or partnership is liable for infringements committed by employees or agents. This liability attaches when the agent acts under the authority or direction of the business, an employee acts within the scope of employment, or the business benefits from, or adopts or approves the infringing activity.

Voir dire (Latin: *speak the truth*). Process by which attorneys and judges question potential jurors in order to determine whether they may be fair and impartial.

Index

Nolo.com offers a large library of legal solutions and forms, created by Nolo's in-house legal editors. These reliable documents can be prepared in minutes.

Create a Document Online

Incorporation. Incorporate your business in any state.

LLC Formation. Gain asset protection and pass-through tax status in any state.

Will. Nolo has helped people make over 2 million wills. Is it time to make or revise yours?

Living Trust (avoid probate). Plan now to save your family the cost, delays, and hassle of probate.

Provisional Patent. Preserve your right to obtain a patent by claiming "patent pending" status.

Download Useful Legal Forms

Nolo.com has hundreds of top quality legal forms available for download:

- bill of sale
- promissory note
- nondisclosure agreement
- LLC operating agreement
- corporate minutes
- commercial lease and sublease
- motor vehicle bill of sale
- consignment agreement
- and many more.

More Bestselling Books

Patent It Yourself
Your Step-by-Step Guide to Filing at the U.S. Patent Office

Patent, Copyright & Trademark
An Intellectual Property Desk Reference

How to Make Patent Drawings
A *Patent It Yourself* Companion

Getting Permission
Using & Licensing Copyright-Protected Materials Online & Off

The Public Domain
How to Find & Use Copyright-Free Writings, Music, Art & More

Every Nolo title is available in print and for download at Nolo.com.

www.nolo.com